This book is for you if..

You are ready to embrace change in your life,
  but could do with a little help

You are ready to start a new business,
  but are frightened to take the leap

You know you are capable of greater things,
  but you feel there is something holding you back

You need to re-energise and grow your business

You need to reinvent yourself and strike out in a new direction

You have realised that if you keep on doing what you are doing, you will keep on earning what you are earning - and it's not enough!

If you are truly ready to take action and achieve your full potential, then you have come to the right place.

This book is for you!

Paul Wakefield Named as Northumberland's StartUp Britain Local Business Champion

North East marketing consultant and internet entrepreneur Paul Wakefield has been named as Northumberland's StartUp Local Champion by national enterprise campaign StartUp Britain.

Paul, who runs digital media projects including the Digital Youth Enterprise and Making U Social, will be using his position to help develop the work he already does to support the growing number of start-ups and SME businesses in the county by organising regular workshops and networking sessions as well as lobbying [the Northumberland County Council] on issues facing businesses within the region.

Paul said: "I'm delighted to have been chosen as StartUp Local Champion for Northumberland. I set up my first business in 2007, and now I'm addicted! I want to use my knowledge to help extend the enterprise work I do with start-ups and SMEs. Help and support in early stages can mean the difference between long-term success and failure.

"Northumberland's business community needs all the help and support it can get so it can grow and flourish in these difficult economic times. Being the StartUp Local Champion means I can offer advice and guidance as well as encouraging others to have the confidence to consider going it alone and starting the business they have always dreamed of."

Campaign founder and director Emma Jones said: "We are really pleased Paul could join our campaign as our local champ for Northumberland. He's already proved he is an accomplished entrepreneur, so it wasn't a hard decision to appoint him!

"He's got exactly what you need as a self-starter – bags of energy, loads of ideas and real can-do attitude. We know he'll do a great job and we wish him every success."

Paul left his job as an Consultant in 2007 and set up in his back bedroom with an old PC and a tiny printer. Since then he has moved the business into a nearby business centre, taking on three new members of staff.

Since 2009 Paul has been written about in a book called 'The Laptop Millionaire', he has trained over 3,500 people from seven different countries via webinars, seminars and workshops, in March 2013 he was listed as a top 100 marketer to follow on Twitter, and has also become a SageUK business expert.

The Wakefield Group was founded by Paul Wakefield when he started bringing together exclusive groups of like-minded entrepreneurs, business people, speakers, consultants, sales people and managers who wanted to increase their reach, maximise their profits and create a better, more rewarding lifestyle.

Paul believes that some marketing strategies work just as well or even better in hard economic times. So, regardless of the ups and downs of the economy, by embracing a full range of marketing communication tools to promote your business, he is confident that with either mentoring, consultancy or guidance, and with hands-on account management, webinars or training workshops, he can show you how to increase incomes, find hidden opportunities, add streams of income, and create smarter, more automated marketing using road-tested methods.

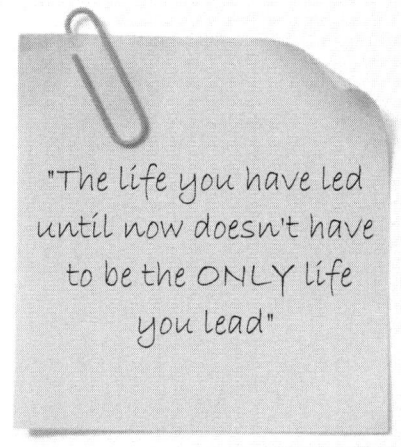

"The life you have led until now doesn't have to be the ONLY life you lead"

"If you keep believing
what you've been
believing,
then you'll keep achieving
what you've been
achieving."

Mark Victor Hansen

What people are saying about Paul

I recently attended the 3 Day Business Makeover from The Wakefield Group and was blown away by the amount and quality of the information which was relayed during that time. My business is already going through changes as a result and I know that the steps we were taught on the course are going to make it so much better in the months to come. Get in touch with Paul to flip your thinking on how to run your business and make a massive difference to your life at the same time!

Amy Purdie

I was a lucky attendee of Paul's 3 Day Business Makeover and it has changed my view on how to run and develop a business. His energy, enthusiasm and knowledge are addictive! I came away from the course with an intense motivation that saw me head straight to the computer to start implementing his advice. I would definitely recommend Paul and The Wakefield Group to anybody wanting to build a successful business.

Paul Bainbridge

It is very clear he knows a massive amount about branding and getting the right message across. He's not afraid to be brutally honest, which I found refreshing. His advice has allowed me to re-brand certain parts of my company for the better, and for that I am forever happy to recommend him to any business owner, big or small.

Ian Wicks

I have known Paul since 2010. He's one of those guys that you know when you meet that he is one to stay in touch with and keep an eye on. What I admire about Paul is that he says it like it is, no hype, no fluff and straight to the point. I always keep an eye out for his updates on Facebook; he is not afraid to say how he feels, even if it does ruffle some feathers. It is this driven and focused outlook in life that has helped him to be as successful as he is. He truly is an inspiration and I would highly recommend following him. I can't wait to read his book!

Aidan Gibson

Paul helped me to see a clarity when we were working together on a group project a few years ago; cuts through the crap and straight to the point - true Brit style. Paul has shown true grit and just got on with it, letting the naysayers go do their own thing. Paul has again proved that unlike certain 'gurus', one does not need to bluff and bluster or mess about; just get down a list of goals, chunk those down to a daily action plan, and get on and 'Just Do It'. I would recommend actually getting on to a workshop of Paul's. Failing that, this book and all the online tools and trainings recommended. Paul has proven his craft with credentials like local government contracts, his online presence and now writing this book, the first of many, I am quite sure.

Ian L Hannaford

It's been interesting getting to know Paul Wakefield over the last few years. Since I first made contact, we have had many conversations about business and personal life. As well as being a very interesting and enlightening down to earth guy, Paul spends the time getting to know you. He is someone who will listen to you and understand you; he has a great wealth of experience in business and personnel development. Paul gets results, he's the sort of person I'd like to have on my team, he is someone you can trust to have on your side. There are so many things I could say about Paul, all in a positive way; you will understand more from reading his book.

Ian Horner

I have recently started working with Paul and have found him to be very professional and client focused. He's creative in his work and will put together the most effective way to build your business online and to help your business generate the leads you want for your industry. I am looking forward to working with Paul closely in the future and can highly recommend him to anyone whose business needs a boost online.

Sonya

Thanks for your support Kelly

NO EXCUSES NO LIMITS!

PAUL WAKEFIELD

Inspirational speaker and
Start Up business mentor

All the Best

Published by
Filament Publishing Ltd
16, Croydon Road, Waddon, Croydon,
Surrey, CR0 4PA, United Kingdom
Telephone +44 (0)20 8688 2598
Fax +44 (0)20 7183 7186
info@filamentpublishing.com
www.filamentpublishing.com

© Paul Wakefield 2014

The right of Paul Wakefield to be identified as the author of this work has been asserted by him in accordance with the Designs and Copyright Act 1988.

ISBN - 978-1-910125-13-7

Printed by Berforts Information Press
Stevenage & Hastings

This book is subject to international copyright and may not be copied in any way without the prior written permission of the publishers.

Contents

Introduction		13
Chapter One -	Goals and Distractions	51
Chapter Two -	Having a Vision of Success	69
Chapter Three -	The Truth about Making Progress Fast	97
Chapter Four -	The Opportunity is There - you just need to take it	113
Chapter Five -	Health as a Means of Efficiency	127
Chapter Six -	Personal Perception	145
Chapter Seven -	We've Come to the End of the Line	161

Summaries

Summary One	169
Summary Two	171
Summary Three	173
Summary Four	175
Summary Five	177
Summary Six	179

Last Word	181
The Importance of Goals	183
How to Simplify your Life	188
The Power of Gratitude	190
Secrets to Staying Happy	192
How Peace of Mind can help you Create Prosperity	195
How to Become More Positive to Attract a Better Life	197
How do Millionaires Set and Achieve Their Goals?	199

Paul Wakefield

"The same winds blow on us all.
The winds of change,
of market forces, taxation
and government.
But is it not the winds that
determine the course of our
lives or our business.
It is the philosophical
set of our sails."

Jim Rohn

No Excuses, No Limits

Acknowledgements

I would like to thank a few people who have stuck with me, supported me and inspired me on my journey into business and in life.

I would like to say a massive thank you to my family, my mum, pops, my sister and my two nans, who have stuck by me throughout my journey.

Sadly, 2009 was the worst year ever having dealt with seven funerals, which sadly included my nans and my two step-granddads, who I miss massively. I honestly believe most families would have been ripped apart by this, yet my family got stronger. My parents are more than just parents to me; they are my mentors, role models, but more importantly, they're my best friends and I wouldn't be where I am right now without them.

I would like to say thank you to Chris Day of Filament Publishing Ltd for helping in making this book happen.

And also the entrepreneurs who most inspire me, but who I don't know personally...

Sir Richard Branson, Peter Jones CBE, Steve Jobs, Deborah Meaden and Michelle Mone OBE.

Finally, I would like to thank Andrew Reynolds for teaching me another way to look at business, and a huge thank you to Nick James who over the years has become a friend as well as a mentor to me.

Paul Wakefield

"Once I discovered what I'm about to share with you, it changed my life forever..."

What I discovered has helped me through some of the toughest times of my life ... Financially ... Emotionally ... Personally ...

In fact, it inspired me to set up my own business ... it has also allowed me to meet and work with some really inspirational people from around the world...

I'm now in a position which allows me to share the very same information with you for FREE...

No Excuses, No Limits

Hello!

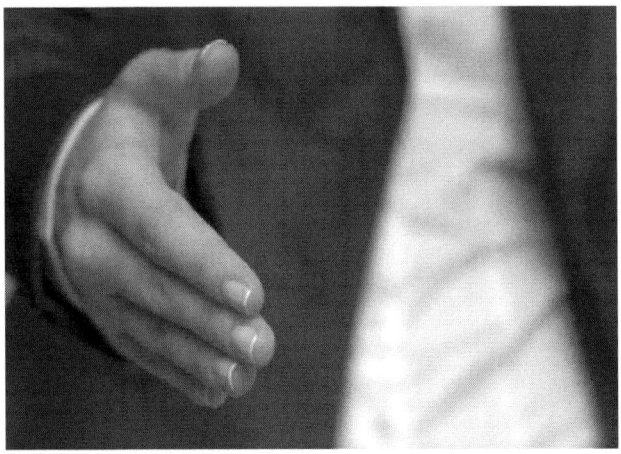

My name is Paul Wakefield...

The life I have... the information I possess ... is all thanks to another little book I read in 2006, and even to this day, it sits at the side of my bed where I can read it again and again and again.

And NO, I'm not some crackpot. Far from it in fact. I'm just an ordinary guy from the UK ... a loving father... a respected businessmen... in fact, a very level-headed man in his thirties who has a story to tell.

A TRUE STORY ... AN AMAZING STORY!

Maybe the most compelling and remarkable story you've ever heard...I hope so! It is a story which relates to something very personal to me which happened only a few years ago and I believe it's all thanks to what I'm about to share with you today that I find myself having such an incredible life...

Now when I stumbled upon this it totally changed my life.

Paul Wakefield

This has bought me more Love, Happiness and Freedom than I could ever of dreamt of... an incredible lifestyle that just keeps getting better and better every single day.

Why this works, I must be honest and tell you I do not know. How to make it work, THAT I do know. Yet still to this day after all I have achieved ... all I have seen ... even after everything it's brought me and everything it still brings me ... I am just stunned. It's pretty amazing stuff!

In 2006, I started my journey into Personal Development; I was told about this small, rather insignificant looking book that had changed the life of who at the time was my boss and thousands of others from around the world.

He told me to go get myself a copy of what he described as "An Incredible Life-Changing Read" ... Now I'm NOT one for reading, I'll be honest with you, so roughly four to five months after first buying this book, I decided to take it to work and read it on my lunch break. It was as though some sort of ageless wisdom had been handed to me and I felt that what I had been waiting for my whole life, which I instinctively knew was out there somewhere, had finally reached me. I now had what I needed to change my life.

Little did I know, at the time, the fundamental shift it would bring... from leaving my nine to five corporate job, to sorting out my personal and financial turmoil.

Now I know what this sounds like!

Believe me, I really do. I know if someone had told me something like this existed a few years ago, I wouldn't have believed it either. I couldn't possible have, certainly not from the dire place I found myself in life...

No Excuses, No Limits

November 2007, I had just lost a lovely two-bedroom house ... split up with my fiancée ... I was out of work and on the dole for the first time in my life ... I was sleeping on the floor in the spare room of a friend's flat ... I hadn't seen my daughter for three years ... in fact, I was at such a low point I decided to go and live in Tenerife and run away from everything. Even that didn't work; I was back within 10 days because I fractured my foot. Everything was going wrong ... but this was the start of something very special. I had so much time on my hands ... I was for the first time in my life able to reflect on everything that had happened to me, everything that I thought was so bad turned out to be so AMAZING...

I spent three months on crutches and three months writing a Business Plan, and went on to set up my Own Business...

Suddenly, I found myself in a lovely newly-built two-bedroom luxury apartment with electric gates at the entrance and an amazing en-suite bathroom in the master bedroom. I was also back in touch with my daughter.

Paul Wakefield

I had suddenly realised that although I thought my life was so BAD, it WASN'T! I got through everything because I remembered ONE crucial part of the book, and that was to STOP making EXCUSES and to be GRATEFUL for everything I had in my life.

For someone who's only 36 (while writing this book), I have dealt with 13 funerals, due to losing friends and family since I was 21 ... In fact, my 21st birthday started with me sat in a church at a funeral.

2009, between February and December, my family and I had seven family funerals to deal with ... I lost my 4 grandparents, my mum's cousin, another relative and a very close family friend all within 10 months ... I'm NOT telling you this for sympathy, I'm simply saying at the age of 36, I have experienced enough in my lifetime, which I know without this information, I would be in a very different place to what I am in NOW ...

As you read on, please understand I am NOT saying any of what now follows to sound flash or to show off. Far from it. I'm just an average man from an average family, something which is very important to me and I am very GRATEFUL for this. So, I assure you I ONLY mention what follows so you can know for sure that I am a GENUINE person ... a REAL person ... and that this really does WORK!

You see, what I'm writing in here and sharing with you has taken me from near poverty and depression to a life where ...

I'm truly GRATEFUL for every penny I have earnt and everything that I have, because in 2007 I can remember going to my bank account and my balance read £2.87. Look, I'm NOT saying I'm a millionaire now but what I am saying is what I learnt from this has made me financially comfortable...

I have become respected in business to such an extent that I have been a volunteer Business Mentor for the Prince's Trust and a Business Mentor for The Young Enterprise Group... something I never imagined would ever happen to someone like me...

In October 2009, I was invited by my mentor, a multi-millionaire, to his Entrepreneur Boot camp at the O2 Arena in London to help raise money for the Make A Wish Foundation. This raised over £700,000 and every penny went to charity. I was lucky enough to be a part of it.

I now have as much FREEDOM in my life as I could ever dream of ... I can do the things I really love doing when I want to and I can work when I want to. I'm NO longer travelling and working around the clock for someone else to have all the financial rewards. I'm NOT saying this information will change your life straight away and I'm certainly NOT saying it's some sort of magic trick. What I am saying is if you follow everything that myself and others have learnt from this, your life can be exactly what you want it to be...

Yet behind all of this... behind all the wonders I have witnessed ... I held a secret. A secret which has directed my life and given me so much more. A secret which has enabled me to experience all these wonders.

But as I said, I'VE ALWAYS KNOWN WHAT THIS SOUNDS LIKE ... as if a secret could even exist. Would people even believe me?

However, it's something which has been playing on my mind recently because prior to beginning my own journey when I stumbled across something TRULY REMARKABLE, my own life was a mess. A complete and utter disaster. Financially, Personally, Emotionally and Physically ... and in a way I wouldn't wish on anyone.

Paul Wakefield

What's in this book I hope will change your entire life forever!

Let me warn you in advance. What you're about to read is not your ordinary, old, dragged through a hedge backwards, overused, oversold and overstated self-help book that contains a load of fluff about how you should live your life through magic, praying, mystical powers or mantras. While some of these methods may work for some, I've been there, I've done that. As far as buying these books, courses, audios and videos go, If it's out there and being sold, it's a safe bet I've studied and thoroughly tested the concepts and techniques in my constant quest for heightened understanding, knowledge, improvement, efficiency, and lots, and lots, of money.

I'm writing this book today with the hope that someone out there that's as eager as myself, constantly striving for success stumbles upon it, and saves themselves years of testing, years of trying the dud methods and utterly wasting their time.

So, what's controversial about this? Well, throughout this book, I'm going to be talking about a lot of things that people do not want to hear. It'll be like an icy cold wake-up call for those who stick with it.

I'm getting ahead of myself already though.

Let's begin with what you're about to experience with this book. That's the most important thing right now. I'm going to give you a quick run down through this introduction section about what's to come, how to use the information, and what makes this book entirely different to anything else out there.

If you want to skip it and get straight to the meat of the book, feel free. As you're about to find out, my rules for success are very lax compared to those harsh regimes you've probably read about. The whole 'You must do this every day, 15 minutes a day, to see results' doesn't suit my personality at all. I don't fancy brainwashing myself to think things are better than they are. My mind needs to be fresh, crystal clear, and imperatively in touch with reality.

Because of this, this was the start of me finding out...

The Difference Between Success and Failure

Paul Wakefield

> Ok, so we all have excuses in life right?! ...

I'm not doing my homework because...

I'm not going out today, because...

I couldn't make the interview, because...

My battery died on my phone, so I couldn't...

It's raining, so I cant...

I missed the bus, so I couldn't...

I don't want to work, because...

> Imagine this...

No Excuses, No Limits

Imagine what it would be like if you looked out on the vast ocean and didn't see any water. Now think about how you would feel if you never saw a star. What would the world be like if there was no music? What if, tomorrow, all the trees were gone, every blade of grass, and every plant and flower dried up and blew away?

What would the world look like then? How would a future artist ever paint a landscape? Where would we be if there were no animals? What would you eat if there were no fruits and vegetables? How many salads can you make with dirt?

Look, we take the world for granted, this life, and this wonderful place where we live. We have everything and more than we could ever ask for. Think about it?! Every last grain of sand. Every plant and every animal, every fish and every seed that we have access to every day, things that we take for granted, things that we need to survive.

If the people who give us these things made EXCUSES every day on why they shouldn't share such things with the world... We wouldn't even be here!

Be Grateful. Stop Making Excuses! Start Right Now!

Think of the future you want to have, not just for you, but your family too. Visualise and picture it in your mind. Start feeling good about it, and know that it is yours. Know that you deserve it. Know that the Universe will create it for you in Abundance.

BUT... YOU HAVE TO STOP MAKING EXCUSES!!

Paul Wakefield

OK, let's get started... As I've already mentioned, this book is the kind of self-help book aimed, quite frankly, at anyone...

It is a must-have book if you're the typical person who every day, or at least every other day, makes EXCUSES on why you shouldn't do this, or do that, or do whatever it is you don't want to do.

You'll soon see this book is written in a different style to most. I'm the kind of guy who is honest, brutally so, sometimes to my own detriment. I'm always getting told I'm very controversial and a lot of people never know how to take me, until they get to know me and my story.

So, I really hope you'll find that I'm true to my values and as a result, honest to you, the reader.

You'll find stuff in this book which makes so much sense that you'll find yourself nodding in agreement. You'll also find a lot of things that you'll find yourself thinking, 'Is this really true?' In this book, we'll be looking at life in a way most people don't and wouldn't even think about looking at in such a way.

Allow me to start by asking you two very quick questions. When was the last time you made a resolve to achieve something, set a deadline, and then achieved it? Can you even remember the last time? If I'm right in saying this, I bet you're struggling. And the reason you are struggling to remember such a time is because of excuses. We make them for everything; consciously and unconsciously. Without noticing it, excuses have become a habit that we struggle to shake off.

In this book, I want to talk about the excuses culture that we have developed within ourselves and why we use excuses to protect ourselves from feelings of failure and fear. Hopefully, it will spur you on in to taking action, becoming someone who stops making EXCUSES, someone who becomes more motivated, starts setting and achieving goals, goals that can make you happier, goals that can make you money and goals that allow you to give back to those you love, goals that allow you to live the life that you deserve.

As I said earlier, I promise you I'm no crackpot. I'm just ordinary guy from the UK, a loving father, a son, a brother, a respected businessman and a level-headed man in his thirties who has a story to tell.

I'm just a working class lad who's often told I have a unique approach to life. Throughout my life, I've made some very bad decisions and excuses. More recently though, I've made some pretty cool decisions but I also make excuses.

I'm hoping that this book will make you understand that making excuses has to STOP. I'm hoping this book will take you from inaction because of all your excuses, to taking action and getting of your backside and stop feeling sorry for yourself, because it's simply not an option. Understand? Right, that's you told, so let's get on. Let me share my story and let's have some fun. However, before we get into too much detail, I'll give you a quick CV of my life.

Paul Wakefield

You might already have learned a little about me, but here it is: My life in a nutshell...

T his is me, aged seven...

So, why aged seven and not a baby picture?

Before I start telling you more about me, when I started writing this book and thinking about the story and how it will start, I could only think about my life from the age of seven... I think I know why this is, and as you keep reading, you will find out why too.

I'm Paul Wakefield, born in High Wycombe, Buckinghamshire on 5th March 1977.

No Excuses, No Limits

Flashes of brilliance, a life of excuses, massive failings, dole, penniless, loyal friend, leader, marketing genius, business development expert, business owner, mentor, consultant, coach, publisher, dad, son, brother and a genuine guy who likes to help others.

While at school between the age of 13 and 16, I had two jobs. I was selling programmes at my local football club, Wycombe Wanderers, earning £10 per match. I also had a paper round delivering a local newspaper called the "Star" and I delivered 750 papers on a Friday, earning £55 a week.

Sadly, during my last two years of school, I was very heavily bullied by my so-called friends. Friends who I'd grown up with all my life. I can remember running home from school and being so scared of what might happen to me if I hang around. I used to come home from school and cry my eyes out.

I remember two occasions very clearly. One was on a Friday afternoon while I was out doing my paper round. One lad, who had been bullying me for some time, came after me with a big kitchen knife. I'd never been so scared in my life. Luckily at this age, I was a very fast runner. I can remember running straight to a friend's house praying all the way that he was in so that I would be safe.

The other occasion was on a Thursday night after youth club. I was on my way home with a group of friends. I'm not sure how, but suddenly a message had got to myself and my group of friends that these people were out and were coming to get me.

I kind of took this message with a pinch of salt and just carried on walking home. Within minutes, seven people had found out where I was, and again I found myself running for my life.

Paul Wakefield

Now you may be thinking two things right now. One, that I'm a wimp for running away, and two, why were these people bullying me.

The truth is they were jealous of me. As I've already mentioned, I come from a very small but very close family. My mum worked part-time as cashier for a very well-known high street bank for about 32 years and my dad was a factory worker, an upholsterer, and a very good one at that. So, you can see by this that both my parents had what I would call an 'average job', certainly nothing that made my parents financially wealthy. Yet I was always looked at as mummy and daddy's little rich boy and that's what people didn't like.

When I left school, I wanted to be a fashion designer, and for whatever reason, my career advisor told me to get into engineering so I tried my hand at being an engineer. After three years of hard work at college and working through my five year apprenticeship, I was told I was dyslexic and to consider a new career.

I'd just wasted three years of my life doing something that I didn't want to do in the first place. I only done it because my career advisor told me to try it. Let's face it, these people are the so-called experts so, of course, I was going to listen to her.

I soon found myself, at the age of 19, working in the clothes shop River Island. I only started off part-time … 16 hrs a week, in fact, helping out in the stock rooms when they had deliveries.

Two and a half years later, I ended up leaving River Island, where I had been promoted over the years and had become an Assistant Store Manager looking after a team of 12 staff.

So, why did I leave, you may ask…

No Excuses, No Limits

Well I was now 19, nearly 20, and a lot of people and friends I knew had either been or were going to work abroad and I liked the sound of that, so off I went to go work in Nerja, Costa del Sol. Sadly, this ended up being a four-week holiday instead due to the weather of tropical storms. Nothing opened up and I ended up coming home to High Wycombe... without a job.

I soon found myself as a trainee car salesman working for a garage called Delta Motor Company, a franchise of Renault with a basic salary of £5,000 a year plus company car.

Eighteen months down the road and this was the start of a very crazy working career, and what I believe to be a life-changing incident too.

Sadly, my 21st birthday was spent at a funeral, and then what followed was awful. Within the next five months, I had another siz funerals, all of which were friends. Friends that I had grown up with and friends that I had got to know as I was getting older.

Paul Wakefield

Out of respect to their families, I'm not going to mention any names, but after experiencing this, I ended up getting counselling for about four years. I suddenly found myself being extremely fearful of life. Apart from one, the friends I had lost were all younger that me and I couldn't handle the fact that friends were being taken from me at such an early age.

As I'm sure you can imagine, this wasn't easy for me to deal with. Now out of respect to my parents, I'm going to keep this brief, but at this point in my life, I was smoking a lot of weed and I had experimented with other drugs too. I was 21, and like most 21 year olds, I was out drinking most nights as well. I wasn't causing any harm to anyone, but I was abusing my body with things that I shouldn't of.

I don't know what made this happen, but this also led to me having my very first panic attack. This panic attack was so bad that my parents had to call an ambulance as I had collapsed in their bathroom. I'm now 36 and I've dealt with anxiety and panic disorder ever since.

Anyway, let's get back to my dreadful working career. I ended up leaving Renault as I was headhunted by a company called Supagard. I'll keep this next bit short as I don't want to bore you so early into the book.

My career in short...

Sales Rep – Supagard (Lasted about eight months. I got the sack)
Orange mobile phone shop (Salesman – Branch Manager)
4 x Pubs (Barman – Pub Manager)

This had to stop, but I didn't really know what I wanted to do. I had to sit back and have a serious think about what I wanted from life and where I was going ...

No Excuses, No Limits

The answer I came up with was that ... "I WAN LOTS OF MONEY" ... "I WANT TO BE SOMEONE" ... "I WANT TO HAVE SUCCESS" ... "I ENJOY HELPING OTHERS" but what could I do that would give me all of this?

No one could tell me and I certainly didn't know ...

I then went back to Renault ... luckily, I had a successful career working for them. I went from a Trainee Salesman to a Business Manager leading a team of 8 staff...

This then went on to me starting my first business. I set up my very own Recruitment Agency specialising within the Automotive Industry...

I thought I had cracked it. I thought this was the start of my dreams coming true and getting everything I had always wanted.

Over the years, I have been very lucky. I've travelled extensively thanks to the hard work of myself and my parents treating me as a kid. I have worked with and met some amazing and inspiring people over the years, and I have built a reasonably comfortable lifestyle for myself.

Paul Wakefield

But this wasn't enough for me...

In 2008, I took time to reflect on what I really wanted from life ... how to use my skills and experience to help others.

I made the decision to move on from a traditional corporate life and build my own home-based business with the control, flexibility and lifestyle benefits that are really important to me. I had enough of intense commuting and exhausting business travel...

... I was no longer prepared to make personal family sacrifices.

I am now committed to helping consumers and businesses, who want to find more personal freedom and lifestyle flexibility, and support them to achieve their goals and aspirations.

I live in a gorgeous part of the UK called Northumberland, where I moved to in 2005. I'm a keen sportsman with golf, football and general fitness featuring in my life. I love to travel and have fallen in love with India.

No Excuses, No Limits

Get Rich Quick!

Before establishing my business, I earned an OK income, but certainly not enough to allow me to spend the time with my family and friends in the way that I wanted to live. So, I took the decision to explore the world of home-based businesses. I took the time to look at loads of different opportunities. I wanted to find a business that enabled me to put my family priorities first and yet still give me the chance to earn a decent income.

There's a lot of rubbish out there that's full of over-hyped promises of great wealth and sure-fire ways to easy riches, i.e. terrible GET RICH QUICK SCHEMES.

I went through a ton of information, websites and searches, and I decided that one really important thing for me was to find somebody already living a successful business life.

Paul Wakefield

I wanted to work with someone who could guide me into this industry and who could help me make a success in the world of either consultancy, coaching, internet or direct marketing and passive income opportunities.

I'm thrilled with the results and I'm now working with some truly successful entrepreneurs earning very significant incomes.

With the help of my mentor, one of UK's most successful Business Mentors creating a £60+ million lifestyle for himself within just 12 years, I was able to learn fast. What could have taken years, took only months. Andrew's guidance and others has enabled me to avoid many of the pitfalls out there and my progress has been hugely rewarding.

Through Andrew's efforts, I soon learnt what works and not waste more time and money on things that don't work. This is where most people fail because they can't learn fast enough; they simply find and use every possible EXCUSE they can think of. They run out of money before they figure out what works for them; they simply get fed up with learning and want everyone else to do it all for them. Don't let this happen to you, because as soon as you STOP making EXCUSES and get it right, you will be enjoying your time and money the way you want to.

What has driven me to this point is that I want to be able to exercise flexibility, personal control and to spend time with my loved ones, because I, perhaps like you, have sacrificed these things in earlier years in order to get to this point in my life.

So, I made a decision that I am no longer going to trade my time for money. I want to use my experience, skills and background to help you deliver unimaginable success.

No Excuses, No Limits

OK, so now I've explained that, can I make one thing very clear here before you continue reading? I'm not a religious person, and I have nothing against other self-help books. What I have got against them is their laid-back attitude. Most can't get it to work, and those that do, don't understand how it works, so I'm going to lay it all on the table for you right now so that you can understand exactly what's going on. Not all of these books and publications are bad either; I'll show you how to tell what's what in a moment. In addition, I suggest reading this whole section before coming to any conclusions about what I'm sharing with you in my book because there are some big exceptions to these rules.

First up, self-help. The whole concept that you can get whatever you like, whenever you like. All you have to do is imagine it and sit back, or think positive. What crap! You think that if you carried out all this stuff and laid on your bed for a month doing nothing, having your food, drink and any other needs catered to by someone else, mantras and hocus pocus would bring you all you want if you ask for it, chant for it, or write it down? Sounds a bit stupid when I put it like that, but ultimately that's what a lot of these books teach.

The most popular ones saying things like, 'Sit back and relax, everything you've ever wanted will come to you.'

It's hardly surprising that when it comes to real life, so many people make EXCUSES after reading rubbish like that.

It pains me to see people using these and seeing positive results. What they don't ultimately understand is that it's not their manifesting, chanting and mantras that got them what they wanted; it was them. This robs the users of these books and courses of something very important – Belief in themselves.

When they achieve something they've always wanted after reading one of these things, what do they say? Thank you (insert cosmic entity here). What happens when they hit their next downer? They can't get up. I've seen it hundreds of times. I used to try and tell people that they won't have the strength to soldier on and fight to achieve something if they don't wake up and realise it's them achieving these great things, but they don't want to listen, so I gave up wasting my time on 'the brainwashed' as I call them.

What happens a month later? I see them whining about how things have started to go badly, or how they've lost everything they've gained. Why? Because they weren't ready to understand what it takes to keep such lifestyles, riches and top of the tree social situations. As soon as a problem came up and things didn't go their way, they can't draw on their confidence in themselves and what they've achieved before and claw their way back up the ladder. This happens all the time in these situations. It happened to me once (thankfully I had my parents to show me what was going wrong), it happens to my friends every day, and I can see it coming from a mile off. Try and put yourself in my shoes for a moment. I'm sure you've experienced this before - You know how when you've learned something and mastered it over a number of years? Something you're really good at.

Maybe it's business or maybe it's a hobby, a sport you took up professionally, even something as simple as using a computer or learning how to play a game or use a new programme. Whatever it is, you're the best at it. Everyone around you knows it and you know it.

One random day, you see someone that mentions they want to do what you're doing. Suddenly your mind is assaulted by a million thoughts and memories about what you went through on your journey; the journey that they're just starting. You wonder if they'll make it, you wonder what you can tell them first; there's so much for them to learn, so many pitfalls to avoid. Not only that, but when you actually see them attempting to do something you've already done successfully, it's almost like you can see what's coming next. If they're heading for disaster and about to do something wrong that will get them into big trouble, you can see it. You know it because you've been there, you've experienced it.

If they're going to succeed or have done something right, you can see it. You know it, because you've been there, seen the sights, understood the concepts, felt the feelings. Your thoughts turn towards whether or not they'll make it through that big spider's web you cut through to success. Are they smart enough? Do they know what to do next? Can they possibly learn and understand what you have?

This, my friends, is how I feel when I see someone take a self-help book to heart. Something that some random person has written, something that the reader sorely wants to believe, and it works. For a bit. I know what's going to happen, because I've seen it. I've experienced it, and I get that same feeling you do when someone takes on a big, long project without knowing what to expect.

Then comes the downfall. The feeling I just described to you is what I see when someone picks up another one of these books. They will not be able to dig themselves out of the big hole they dig themselves into without a difficult fight. For those of us who understand the concepts in this book, we know that when we do something right, and it goes well it was us.

This is the first concept I'd like you to take on board. This is what turned me into who I am today. Reading along now, you might think I'm probably a little cocky, a bit full of myself and not the nicest person in the world. Why? Because every time I'm successful at something, I know that I did it. No one else. No cosmic forces, no wishing, no hoping. Me. That makes me damn good at what I do. The simple fact that I understand this concept is why I can tell you if anything goes wrong, I'll be back. If I lost everything today, I wouldn't be chanting or buying self-help books or anything like that. I'd be getting out there and getting back on top through my actions. Something that the self-helpers don't get.

No Excuses, No Limits

When you stop making EXCUSES and start believing in yourself, this is the first key to success. It is the number one point that I have written in my diary, and from the moment I took it on board, well, you can see what happened. Confidence is the key factor. That's the only good thing about those 'sit back and relax' books. It gives people confidence (to begin with, anyway). It's just not viable long-term.

But what if you don't have that confidence? Throughout my life, I've extensively studied people who lack confidence. In fact, this subject came up again less than two weeks ago when I was watching someone go through a stage of total lows, and was just emerging from the other side, gathering pace and confidence as she went. It was really amazing to watch and in fact, because it was a close friend, be a part of in some ways. In addition, it involved her business and financial situation in a big way, so it interested me even further than usual. Yet again though, the correlation was there. It was the same as I'd previously seen in all other major happenings that I'd tracked, and the minor entries I'd made.

The first step to her digging herself out of this rut was simply this. When she did something good, profitable, efficient, extraordinary, or just something that moved her a step closer out of the rut she was in, she actually recognised it.

We've already established it's almost impossible to get anywhere without at least a little bit of confidence, but do you think people who have low or no self-confidence and always seem to be down on their luck never do anything good, or never achieve anything worth noting? Of course they do, and that is their first opportunity to get themselves moving forward at blinding paces and make progress like they've never experienced it before, but only if they recognise what they've done. Most people do not recognise their achievements because they're too busy making excuses about other things.

Paul Wakefield

They're so used to waiting for someone else to tell them they've done well, that unless that happens, they don't see it. With all that jealousy, hate, anger and frustration swilling around the everyday world, now our innocent school days are gone, we cannot rely on someone else to say something. We have to recognise our achievements ourselves. Life has shown me that if I ever strike a low and I'm not achieving my full potential, I need to begin to recognise when I've done something good. And so do others. No matter how small and insignificant it may seem.

At the start of this introductory story in this book, I talked to you about how I got my new luxury apartment. I can tell you now that was an achievement. It wasn't easy. Getting a place in such a short space of time wasn't easy, but that was an achievement too and I was unbelievably proud of how I totally dug myself out of that ditch. Still am.

But you know what, it doesn't have to be something as major as that. I still pat myself on the back when I've taken the plunge and taken a course and learnt something new. My most recent adventure is setting up my second business called Digital Youth Enterprise Ltd in a time when everyone is making excuses about the recession. Not many people would be brave enough. Look around you; people like security. I'm proud of that; I patted myself on the back again.

> *"Optimism is the faith that leads to achievement. Nothing can be done without hope and confidence."*
>
> *Helen Keller*

On the same note, look around you. How many of your friends are doing what you're doing now? There might be the odd one, but if you know a lot of people, or look at those you went to school with, odds are that they're stuck in their jobs and don't like their financial situation or the amount of free time they have.

What are they doing about it? Nothing, they're just making EXCUSES.

What are you doing about it? Well, you're reading this book. You've taken a step into the unknown, brushed all that has come to be known as a 'normal life' aside and taken the plunge. That is a huge step on its own.

My guess is it doesn't seem all that much to you. Either you've been doing it for so long you take it for granted now as normal, and not all that extraordinary, or it just comes naturally to you, and you never really saw it as an achievement. Can you see now when I put it like that, that it actually is? This is what people miss.

They achieve, they work their fingers to the bone, even if they fail they learn something, if they win they reap the rewards, and yet, they still don't recognise it as achieving.

Let's take this down to an even smaller scale. I did the dishes last night, got my hands into all that congealed chicken jelly, scraped it all off, tidied the kitchen and scrubbed until it was pristine. Catch is, I was really tired and just wanted to go to bed, but I did it anyway. I patted myself on the back, because knowing some of the people that I know, my friends, my family and those around me, I can tell you for sure that they would have just left it until the morning, yet I didn't. I achieved. I made progress and I recognised it. Sure that my sound unbelievably insignificant, but actually, if you look closely, it's not. It's the first step to excellence, stepping up to the plate, and doing something, no matter how small, that others would have hidden from. This is where my confidence comes from, and where my recovering friend's confidence comes from now she's begun to recognise her achievements (with no input from me no less, so good on her).

But hold on there, don't get me wrong now. I'm not trying to teach you some smiley happy way of always looking on the bright side. That would be self-defeating. Looking on the bright side all the time that some choose to teach, would be like not being able to feel any pain and accidentally resting your hand on the lit barbecue. You don't notice, you get burned, and end up in intensive care with half a bedraggled hand wrapped up in a burns bag.

If only you could feel the pain, the worst you'd have left with would be a few blisters, because your reflexes tore your limb away from the searing heat before any major damage was done.

Let's keep this simple...

When you do something good, when you break from the norm, when you achieve, when you can honestly say you've done something that someone else can't, won't, wouldn't dare, or is too lazy to do, congratulate yourself. No matter how small it is. Look at every action that you carry out. Don't take it for granted. Don't make an excuse on why you didn't get the results you thought you should of. You must recognise when you do well and not kid yourself when you don't. If you can do this, you're well on the way to personal and business success, quite simply because you know whether to put your hand in deeper, or to pull it away because things are going wrong. Ignoring these feelings are devastating, especially in the example I gave you above. I hope that made it clear where I'm coming from with this too.

Don't worry, I'm not asking you to do anything embarrassing like talk to the mirror, or shout out the window about how you did the dishes late at night when your friends would have just gone to bed and wasted time in the morning when they could have used it for something more productive. Nothing like that. Just step back from what you've done. Have a think about it, think to yourself

'Nice one', Impressive' or 'Awesome.'

Admire your work and bring forth a contented grin. I have no chants or some special line for myself. It changes every time. Just whatever you're comfortable with. It shouldn't feel forced either.

Listen, I don't really mind what you say, what you think, or what facial expressions appear on your face at the time, as long as you stop and recognise your achievements, no matter how small. It's not even something that you have to force yourself to do. You'll see what I mean. Just recognise it, and your reaction will come naturally.

You'll probably even find yourself looking for that feeling when something comes up that you don't really want to do, and you'll go ahead and do it anyway, because you're making progress, and it gives you that comfy fulfilled feeling of having moved another step closer to your goals.

In addition to the above, justify your actions. Look for reasons. Going away and patting yourself on the back or congratulating yourself at every opportunity isn't what we're after here. Reasons help the whole process of easily spotting when you've made progress.

You're patting yourself on the back because 'It was hard, but I did it anyway', 'I didn't feel like it, but I did it anyway', 'Because I'll have more free time tomorrow as a result of what I've just done', 'Because I'm a step closer to finishing this project', 'Because it's the best seven pages I've ever written. It's not just seven pages, it's a good, strong, solid seven pages that someone, somewhere is going to get something from', 'Because I enjoyed it'.

You didn't sit back and make an excuse on why you shouldn't do it.

This makes you super AWESOME!!

If you can't give a reason, you probably shouldn't be congratulating yourself. We must avoid dulling those senses as to what's progress and what's not.

So, there we have it. A simple task followed by a very simple, very real action that you can take, followed by a very strong, totally natural, action inducing reaction you'll get in return. No hocus pocus, cosmic entities, false feelings, dulling your senses, fancy names, or positive thinking needed.

It's just a question of opening your eyes and seeing your real potential being realised step by step, whether it be in your personal life, your daily maintenance, or your business. We have to get personal to be winners, which is why I'm taking this route. You can't see amazing results in one and ignore the other. It all improves under one heading. You and your life.

"Believe in yourself! Have faith in your abilities! Without a humble but reasonable confidence in your own powers you cannot be successful or happy."

Norman Vincent Peale

Paul Wakefield

Let's look at our childhood

As a child, our parents want us to do things, right? After all, that's the only way we learn.

As a child, I remember my parents asking me to do all sorts of things, things that would sometimes only take a few minutes, things that would help my parents. I also remember answering back with a load of EXCUSES on why I hadn't done what I was asked to do. This wasn't because I was cheeky, it was just simply easier to make up an excuse than it was to do what I was asked to do.

Do you remember your parents ever saying this to you?...

"If you had just done it instead of making up excuses, it would be done by now!"

As a kid, I would rather do things I liked doing than take responsibility. To me, everything looked like hard work so I would start doing what I was asked to do then I'd give up.

As kids, we have fantastic EXCUSES on why we don't want to stop playing. We just expect our parents to go along with our fantasies. I mean, let's be honest here, even at the age of seven or maybe even earlier, I'm sure I probably looked at my parents and thought they were daft.

It's a challenge being a kid, right? Look, at the ages of six to nine years of age, we start school. This means getting into a routine at a really young age… I'm 36 and I'm not one for routine now, let alone at the ages of six to nine years old.

Allow me to jump on a few years here...

As children, we need someone to look up to. Normally as children, that's our parents, right? But sadly, so many people in this day and age are less fortunate to have parents to look up to. Does that mean they can go on in life making EXCUSES? In my eyes, no, it doesn't.

It shouldn't be too hard to think of someone that you want to be like, or have the skill of. For example, maybe you want to beat them, or go further than they have in their careers. Excellent; in that case, head on out and grab their autobiographies and training manuals, audio book, whatever it is that's on offer to you. I want to stress this point of athletes and sports players, especially because, let's face it, they've been there, done that… Now imagine if they spent all day, every day making EXCUSES. Truth is, they know how to go from nothing to the top of their game. They've overcome these problems and found solutions already. If you have a favourite sports personality, head on out there and see what they have to teach you.

If you find reading big 800 page autobiographies about someone else boring, grab one anyway, and flick through. Read the odd paragraph here and there, and see what you can pick up.

Remember, you don't have to be a big fan; just someone you admire for their achievements. If you can't think of any sports personalities, then there's lots of business owners out there that have written books about themselves. Of course, there's also lots of other categories; writers, dancers, designers, inventors, innovators, and more. What's important is that all of them will be able to tell you more actionable methods for business and life success, results, efficiency and progress than anyone who thinks making EXCUSES, sitting back, thinking happy thoughts and expecting success to land on their doorsteps is ever going to work for you.

Here's how I believe you could use this book

I've said it already, and I'm going to say it again. How you use this book is entirely up to you. I'm not going to overtly lecture you throughout the whole thing about how you have to do everything written here or this won't work. That entirely defeats the object of the whole thing. Instead, I'm going to give you all the information I have, through my extensive research, data collection, testing, and real life application, show you it absolutely positively works, and leave it all up to you. Don't like something? Great, that's your choice entirely. You don't have to use it. Like something you read? Great, go ahead and put it into action and watch the results roll in.

It's a well-known fact that if you're told you have to do something, or you need to do something, you're going to make EXCUSES. You're going to end up avoiding it, skipping it, and putting it off. The first mistake of the amateur wannabe self-help book writer is telling you what you should and shouldn't do, what you can and can't do, and when you have to do it.

Here, you have a choice

When you're in control yourself and are free to pick and choose what you do and how often, the pressure is off, and often, you'll find that you want to do it. What happens when you want to do something? Not only is it highly likely you'll be massively better at what you do, but you'll also enjoy it, because it's not a chore anymore. You won't make an EXCUSE on why you shouldn't do it.

The first tips are coming out already; consider this one a freebie. Even the most dedicated business owners that look like robots on the outside get more done almost effortlessly when they give themselves the freedom not to do it. At first glance, it sounds like a contradiction. Think about it for a moment though.

When you're done, we'll move on keeping this at the front of your mind at all times: It is your choice... It will continue to be your choice throughout this book and throughout life. Pretty awesome, huh?

So, why this book and not others?

I'm going to keep this one quick and simple, because if you're still here, there's no doubt in my mind that you're eager to get into the main body of the book and get changing the outlook of your life and maybe your business too. So, here it is; five reasons this is different from anything you may have experienced before as far as this genre of books goes.

- ## Reason 1

I'm not going to tell you how to run your life. I will never try to force a piece of information on you, or tell you things like 'If you do/don't do this for 15 minutes a day, you will succeed/fail at everything'. You are in complete control of what you do and when you do it. I will, however, give guidance and suggestions along with my findings, experiments, stories and opinions, so you won't be left entirely in the dark. Follow my rules, or make up your own. It's up to you. I'm simply writing this book to share my story with you.

- ## Reason 2

I've adapted my findings and diary entries to life and business and been testing them over a six-year period (as of writing this book). At least 700 of those 1000+ experiments that I carried out can be applied in life and business situations. I have no interest in changing your personal or social life for you. Although much of what we talk about here will also benefit you in this area, my primary concern is, as advertised, life and business success.

- ## Reason 3

I am not a guru, a doctor, a PhD. I have no special initials or symbols after my name. I am a normal person, who at 19 was told that I'm dyslexic. I started from zero, with a pen and paper. I had no jump-start. I was not born into success and then decided to write a book about how I became successful (which seems to be a common sight nowadays). All of this is an advantage because I now know how to become successful from nothing, unlike many other attempts at this sort of thing from people who got it handed to them on a plate, and suddenly think they're qualified to teach others how to make it big from nothing. You're getting the real deal here. What I'm sharing with you has been a part of my daily life since I was seven years old.

- *Reason 4*

You don't have to wait for it. While I will be talking about attitudes and approaches to specific situations, I won't be focusing on positive thinking. Every single word I write for you is action based. It's something you can act on if you want to, not something you have to sit back and 'wait for it to come to you' like so many teach (just for the record, some of them are right in their approach in my experience; however, they always neglect to talk about action unless it's in the form of meditation, mantras and stuff like that. None of that here. All life and business orientated action).

- *Reason 5*

Practical application. I'm going to be showing you how I integrate all this into my lifestyle and apply it to my business. I will give you directions that you can follow if you choose to implement that particular point and require guidance on how you might do that. Each point we're going to discuss is individual too, so you don't have to plough through the whole thing just to get to where you can apply this stuff.

And there we have it; that's the introduction out of the way. I hope you enjoyed the introduction, and I also hope it gave you some insight into exactly where I'm coming from in my writing and why I'm qualified to be writing this in the first place.

*"Do you want to know who you are?
Don't ask. Act!
Action will delineate
and define you."*

Thomas Jefferson

I hope you've enjoyed the opening, or at least got something out of it that will get you on that road to the lifestyle you want. I also hope you can excuse my abrasive attitude – I assure you, I'm the nicest person you'll ever meet in real life. I keep all of this to myself, because as you can see, when it does come out, it doesn't always sound particularly polite, proof that confidence doesn't make you unsociable, cocky or rude in real life, even if that's your mindset (more on changes later). My teaching methods do tend to be rather blunt though. People remember them and take action far more often that way, which is why I do it. I'll keep the bad language to a minimum, of course, for those of you out there who don't appreciate that.

Disclaimer

Lastly before you bolt off and get started with the real story...

I have strong views. Some of you won't agree with me on various things, some are controversial, but in my experience all work. I've passed them on to 3,531 people from seven different countries since 2009 alone and it worked for those that would listen. Now, I pass it on to you. Do with it what you will, but don't let your preconceptions and opinions hold you back. There's going to be a lot of breaking the mould with this book, and you're likely to be at the centre of the whole thing.

... but remember one thing, YOU must at least read this book once all the way through. Don't make any EXCUSES and put it down.

CHAPTER ONE

Goals and Distractions
Planning Your Future

OK, I'm going to give it to you straight. The first thing we're going to talk about in this section is setting goals. As you can see in this picture, I completed my first half-marathon in 2012. Every year from 2005, I kept saying that I would do it, but every year I made an EXCUSE on why I wouldn't. Enough was enough. I had to stop making EXCUSES and commit myself to doing it. I'm proud to say that I raised just over £300 for Oxfam and completed the 13.1 miles in just over three hours.

I digress. Let's get back to setting goals. It's old, it's cliché but it's always far from boring, especially as this is one of the few moments where you get to talk entirely about yourself without anyone getting bored or butting in with their own experiences. This is something for you.

It should be private and as personal as you want it to be, or as business orientated as you want it to be.

You wouldn't be mistaken in noticing that this is the basis of most performance enhancing books that I rained on so heavily in earlier chapters. Let it be known, I have no problem with setting goals, and it works. It works well. Once you write something down and place it somewhere memorable or in full view, it's very hard to get that picture of your brand new car, new house, mountains of money or luxury lifestyle out of your mind. This is what's going to spur you on when things aren't going so well, and make you do even more when things are going well.

So, I'm going to jump straight into another task. Here it is:

Grab yourself a piece of paper and set down your goals for the future. You can do this as short-term or as long-term as you like. Whether you have a to-do list that you cross off every day, or something more long-term, I'd suggest starting with a much longer term outlook. Where do you want to be in a month, six months, a year, two years and five years? What belongings do you want to have? Who do you want to know? Write it all down.

Oh, and something that I think is neglected in usual goal setting methods, is the ability to visualise what you want. Not because visualising will make it land in your lap without you having to lift a finger, but instead, because when you do need to look at those goals to be inspired and spurred on, it's far easier when you can get a clear picture of exactly what you want and how it'll feel when you get there.

I'm going to leave this one totally up to you. Write them down, using as many descriptive words as you want.

No Excuses, No Limits

Have a bit of fun with it if you like; get pictures of houses, cars and luxury items from the internet, magazines, and get them alongside your text to help you see where you're going. Remember, I'm not asking you to shout it from the rooftops. No one is going to see this but you, so be as crazy as you like.

Stick it to your fridge, put it in a book of goals, keep it on the computer, put it under your pillow, whatever you want to do with it; it's entirely your choice. Writing them down in the first place makes it real though, and is the most important part of the whole process, fancy names not needed. Goals. Enough said.

Let me tell you a bit of a secret now that no one knows (aside from me). I have my own personal book of goals sitting next to my bed next to my most prized possession (my diaries, if you didn't guess).

It's a handmade leather book from India. On each page there is a goal, a picture that I can easily relate to the goal, the date I came up with it, and the date I achieved it.

What can I say? It works. I look forward to crossing off things from that book. Before I had it, I was making progress, but since I began with it, it's much easier to work out not only what I want, but which path I should tread to get them – my priorities. Words can be inspiring by themselves, but put a picture alongside a powerful descriptive paragraph, and it takes on a whole new format.

Don't want to go to those lengths? Well that's fine. I know how some people feel strange about keeping such things. They think it's weak, or sad, corny, or whatever. At the very least though, goals in order of date to be achieved would be the most advisable course of action to begin with. You can always develop it later on.

Hey, quick tip before we move on.

I find it much better to separate business and personal goals. You'll find out later that if I'm not in the mood to work on my business, I won't. If I am, I do. Separating each one is a must.

Don't get sucked in like I did. Isn't it nice to imagine?

I know we already spoke earlier about where you should head if you want to learn more about performance in business, progress, mindsets and the like, but chances are, if you're here and reading this right now, you may consider researching other methods. I want to warn you in advance what you're going to find along the way in the hope that you won't be taken in by anything that promotes mindset over action and progress through pro-activity (ultimately, that's all it takes).

So, what are you likely to find? Well, to put it bluntly, a lot of people telling you what you want to hear. Listen, marketing and sales is all about playing on emotions. The most powerful forms of marketing target things like jealously, greed, hate, frustration, anxiety, fear, and more. Some of the more skilled marketers will play on love, happiness, bliss, hope, joy and getting things you want with the least effort. All the happy thoughts. The really sly ones will use all of those bundled together to take you on a roller coaster ride, ending with your wallet in their pockets. This is especially true when it comes to books and products created and released in the same light as this one.

Paul Wakefield

Now I know you're not stupid, I know you're not gullible. I'm not suggesting that for one moment. If you were either of those things, you would have dismissed this book ages ago and searched for something that would give you an easier ride.

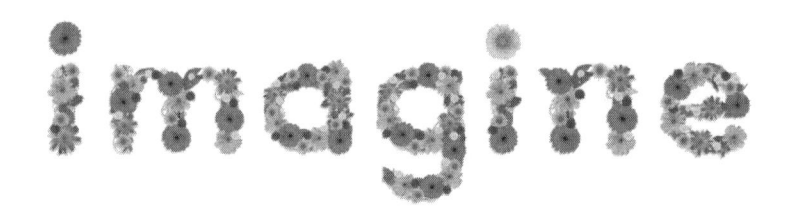

imagine

Imagine if I told you all you have to do is write what you want on a piece of paper, place it under your pillow and you'll get everything you ever wanted. You'll become rich, you'll become good-looking, you'll live the luxury lifestyle. It's so easy, you don't even have to do anything. No stress, no strain, just complete relaxation in your new piles of money. Sounds nice, doesn't it?

We both know that's complete rubbish, but if you land on a particularly website with a well-written sales letter, you may find yourself saying 'What if...' Especially when the place is packed with testimonials from the website owner's friends and those singing its praises everywhere for the short-term help it's given them. (We've already been through the short-term and how I believe these products are devastatingly damaging for the long-term, cutting out vital senses and all logical reasoning that we need to stay on track.)

Don't do it. Try it once if you feel the need, but if you stop to think for just one moment, you'll see how it defies all logic. Everything we learn throughout our lives, and now someone is telling you that you don't even have to do any work to be successful. It's such a powerful marketing tool, catering to eliminating all the negatives and enhancing all the positives in one foul swoop. That's all it is though. Clever marketing.

I found that out a long time ago after I spent, well, wasted thousands of pounds, and I'm passing that information on to you in the hope that you'll be able to keep your head. As the saying goes, if it's too good to be true, it probably is. Keep it in mind when you leave this book and search further afield for more information. Stick with the sportsmen and women, and learn to differentiate between a good book and clever marketing. Be careful out there.

Alright, all done with that now. Apologies for interrupting the flow there. That was for those who might decide to leave us early. For those of you sticking around, let's get straight back to some of the more practical elements my results presented to me.

Why staying focused is a Must
By moving things around

OK, that might sound like a complete contradiction, but I assure you it's not. I'm going to keep this one short, because there's not really a huge amount I need to say to get my point across. Now I don't know about you, but I always find it infinitely easier to concentrate when everything around me is tidy and clean. No TV blaring in my ear, no music playing (unless it's something that helps me concentrate or gets me in the mood for writing). Of course, I'm talking about removing distractions – but only when you feel like it.

Get rid of those TVs, those radios, lock yourself in a room and ask not to be disturbed. Mix in a bit of your favourite music, and you're sorted. I can never get any work done unless I'm in this situation. Problem is, that's a bit boring, isn't it? Sitting in a room all on your own, not really doing much but writing away with nothing particularly interesting to do. Notice I said a moment ago about removing distractions – when you feel like it. This is the key here.

The only time you should have to do this is for maybe an hour a day, max. That's if you work on your business or improving your lifestyle, say, for eight hours throughout that day. Most books will tell you to remove everything and just sit in a corner and don't come out until you've finished. How utterly boring. The only time you should have to do this is when you need to concentrate, and concentrate hard, i.e. when you're planning.

I'll talk to you about planning methods later, because I'll let you into a little something here. The way I write my products, run my business and improve my life, I spend 30 minutes to an hour locked away concentrating hard. I can then spend the next eight hours writing while I watch TV, listen to music and chat on the phone all while creating good products, carrying out customer service ops, designing and building websites, planning and carrying out my marketing, and more.

Can you imagine being locked away in a room for eight hours having to dedicate 100% of your effort and concentration on your business? That's what most do and end up overtired at the end of the day, dreading having to repeat the dull and drab process when they wake up in the morning.

We don't need to do that because we're smarter. I'll explain how to do that later, but for now, another task in preparation for when things get heavy. (You probably noticed I'm going easy on you in this section. I did that on purpose. The sections go Intro, heavy, easy, heavy, easy, heavy and so on, just to give you a bit of a break in-between. Told you I'm not all bad!)

No Excuses, No Limits

Your task, should you choose to accept it, is to dedicate a space for yourself. Let your family know that when you ask not to be disturbed, you really mean it; unless the house catches fire, you don't want anyone or anything near you. This is imperative for the planning process. Next, gather up your favourite music, and put it on your computer or your MP3 player so you're ready for when you give the planning stages a shot. Ditch those distractions now. If you can't keep the TV or the radio off, get rid of them now. If you can't keep away from those computer games, move them out of your dedicated 'do not disturb' space. If you think you could handle keeping them off, leave them where they are. We'll continue talking about this later as that's just basic prep for what's to come. I want to leave this there though and move on to something a little more practical right away.

Why it's Good To Re-Arrange Everything... Embracing Change

Change is good. We all like change, especially if the situation that we're in right now isn't particularly good. The problem is, most people are scared of change. If you could see my diary and my attempts to get people to do things that they've said they wanted to do, expressed interest, it's totally safe, they're full of energy; yet when it's handed to them on a plate, they shy away. Change is all very nice in our minds, but very few of us have the guts to actually go ahead and make it happen.

> "Change your thoughts and you change your world."
>
> Norman Vincent Peale

Paul Wakefield

This is a little exercise I've used since I was quite young to try and root myself out of the boring old 'normal' way of life that everyone seemed to accept as normal. Even to this day, people ask me questions like 'You're always trying new things, and they all work out well', and 'How is it when you try something new, you're always instantly good at it?' or 'I find it weird that here we all are working our jobs and want to change our lives to be like yours, but none of us seems to have the guts to do it… apart from you', (that one turned me a strange plum colour in front of pretty much everyone I know. I like to talk to my friends on the same level, you see, not as someone who thinks he's superior in some way. That one made me sound cocky and I didn't even say anything).

This is what I told them: 'Yeah, what can I say? Change is just exciting to me, always has been'. That was a lie really, but like I said, I don't like discussing my experiments with people I know due to the huge risk of sounding like a cocky know-it-all.

Anyway, I noticed this a long while ago when I was a kid. I always liked the thought of change too, but it took me some time to figure out how I can start to see it as something exciting with a good outcome rather than something scary that could go either way. I started changing my room around when I was about 10. You know the feeling when you've just moved your bedroom around, or when you change the furniture in your house. For a few short days, it has this brand new, pristine aura about it. It's almost like being in a hotel or something.

I don't know about you, but I love that shin[y]
was the first experiment I carried out with regar[d]
seeing it as something acceptable and inviting, and [a]
non-stop. It went down a storm, according to my entr[y]
you remember rightly, I mentioned I never actually put th[e]
to use beyond the actual experiments, which never lasted l[onger]
couple of weeks at the absolute maximum.

As soon as I got my own place, this was one of the first aspects of my diary I put into action. If you come around to see me any time during the day, you'll either catch me a) in the shower or b) changing my furniture around. My original theory was that this is all about embracing change, making it something to accept rather than run away from.

The moment I did this, I started seeing immediate changes. For example, two weeks after I started, I made an unconnected decision to quit my last job and go for something more up my street. My own business. Every single time I stop doing this for over a month, things begin to grind to a halt. Every time I pick it up again and decide that I'm going to continue doing this, something profound happens. This was part of my most recent experiments where I was introducing and removing this over and over again to see what effect it actually had. I quit my job by accepting change; I turned my first business profit by accepting change. I could concentrate harder, for longer, and get 10 times the amount of work done compared to previously. I don't know what it is. Like I said, it's kind of like a hotel feeling, but I guess you could liken it to staying over with friend or relative, or going on holiday with someone. It's so unfamiliar, like someone is watching you.

...ield

...how it is when you're around other people, always on your best ...ur, won't complain about anything and you'll just get on with the ...e moment you get home, it's tear off your clothes, grab a beer out ...ridge, grab a sandwich, slump in a chair and watch TV. OK, so you may ...be that bad, and I have yet to meet anyone who is that bad, thankfully, ...ut you get where I'm coming from. So, why not try it yourself?

Just once, I think, is the ideal name for this optional task. Take a day off, have a quick tidy up, and then move all your furniture in your bedroom or your study, or your whole house if you want (although that could take some time. Just the sitting room, bedroom and study would be ideal). Once you've done it, stand back for a moment and see how it feels. Everything is tidier, cleaner, and feels new, almost pristine.

Remember this feeling, because this is what change feels like.

The biggest problem that business owners have when trying to get a business off the ground is to keep accepting change. They've already done it by deciding to start up their business in the first place, propelling themselves above 99% of the rest of the population. Will they be able to keep it going though? Change happens all the time in business and in life, not just once. Attach a positive feeling to change, and you'll want it more, you'll crave it, and you'll grab it with both hands almost every time it arises, removing the strangest of fears that are innate in all of us. Fear of the unknown.

I thought it might be interesting to tackle the subject of change in more detail, and why it is difficult to change.

Sometimes we welcome change into our lives, but other times we resist and run the opposite direction. Even if we know we need to make a change, it's certainly easier and takes less effort to stay the same.

One of the most important things to realise is that sometimes when we avoid making the changes we want, eventually another person, or life, will make them for us.

It is far more beneficial to create the changes we want, rather than just waiting for something to happen. Like I said, this process is not always easy, but it's definitely a necessary one to embrace. Exploring why it is difficult to change is a good first step. Let's take a look at some of the reasons why change is so hard in the first place:

We are creatures of habit:

For the most part, people need a sense of order and routine. Without these things, there tends to be feelings of confusion and discomfort. On some level, making a change causes a temporary sense of chaos, so it might make you think that you should go back to the way things were, even if you were miserable. Many people start to make changes and then get into a cycle of fear and worry, and avoid what needs to be done. In the end, the hardest part about changing isn't necessarily the change itself, but the anticipation.

> "Better keep yourself clean and bright; you are the window through which you must see the world."
>
> George Bernard Shaw

It's easier to stay the same than to change:

Doing the same thing over and over usually produces the same results, and whether you're happy with those results or not, it's simply easier just to stay the same. However, sometimes you realise you've had enough and it's time to shake things up. You might find you're suffering more than thriving if a change badly needs to be made, and it's irrational to think that things will magically transform without some effort. So, even though it can be unnerving, making the decision to change and jumping in with both feet is a celebration in itself.

We're operating on autopilot:

This is another reason why it is difficult to change. Now, it's not necessary a bad thing to be on autopilot, but it means that you might not notice when a change needs to happen. Many people tend to do things the same way without questioning their actions too much. It's only when patterns are acknowledged and broken that a change can arise.

Change takes effort:

Sure, it's easy enough to set goals and get pumped up for a while, but if you don't put in the honest effort, the changes you want will elude you. Putting in effort means taking small steps every day towards the changes you want to make in life, such as signing up for classes or seminars, doing action-oriented activities, and those big or small steps that lead to achieving goals. In the change process, you have to keep yourself motivated, moving forward, and aware of where you are now and where you want to go.

Fear of the unknown:

Changing brings up feelings of vulnerability and the uncertainty that you're exploring unknown territory, and there is no guarantee how things will turn out. For some people, this part is exciting and invigorating, but others tend to dislike the unknown and prefer the predictable. In the end, diving into the unknown is usually where some of the greatest growth and feelings of accomplishment can happen.

Maintenance
Reactivity vs. Pro-Activity

OK, this is the last easy section before we start getting back into the heavy mind-bending stuff. Don't forget that you don't have to do all of these at once. You can stop, start and jump around wherever, whenever and however you feel comfortable.

Do you ever feel like you've finished for the day, flake out on your sofa and relax just for a moment. 'Wow, I'm tired'. That 'just got home' feeling you get after you've just done a hard day's work. But then you think about tomorrow. Half of the things you've done today will have to be repeated tomorrow and when you think about it, you didn't get all that much done today. If you did, you wouldn't have so much to worry about when you wake up. I know the feeling, and I wouldn't worry too much. You'll be pleased to know it's easily fixable.

This one came about at several points over the course of my diaries, where I studied not only my day, but the day of those around me. What were we really doing with our day to come home feeling so knackered, yet so very far from contented? Do you know how you spend your day? Let's find out, shall we?

Paul Wakefield

Something I noticed very early on in my business career is that most of my day was taken up by maintenance. I'd be cleaning, tidying, organising, getting ready for tomorrow, maintaining, re-designing my sites for my customers, providing them with new content that they weren't even expecting. It was 99% reactive. None of it was really taking me closer towards my goals.

Now, de-cluttering and tidying the place up so it's in pristine condition always made me feel great. I could sit down at the end of day and feel relaxed. You know how it is when you've give the house a once over with the duster and cleaning equipment, dinner is done, eaten up, the dishes cleaned, the sink tidied and put away. You've had a shower and you're ready for bed. How often do you do your big tidy up? I don't know many people who don't do one every couple of weeks or so. Sometimes more often. This is a favourite subject of mine that you may have heard me talk about before in my marketing reports, because it doesn't just apply to real life, but in a business sense too.

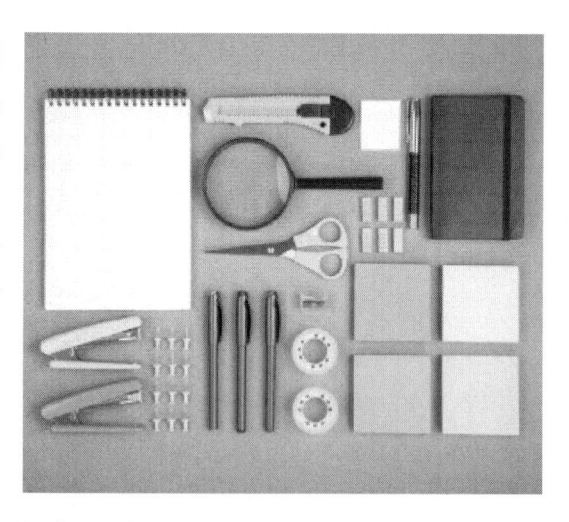

When we're looking for progress, it's important that we can keep track of our days. All that tidying and cleaning should be done on a daily basis. General maintenance every day, instead of one big stint at the end of the week or whenever you have your cleaning days, because otherwise what happens is what I adoringly named Broken Vase Syndrome. My previous customers will recognise this one from my other marketing reports. For those of you who don't know what it is, picture this.

No Excuses, No Limits

You wake up in the morning, get out of bed, have breakfast, jump into the shower after picking up the bills and letters in your mail, which you place on a table in your sitting room. You come out of the shower and open your bills, make yourself a drink, grab the morning's newspaper and have a read. Damn, you forgot to clean up the shower for the next person, so you head on in to give it a quick scrub down.

On heading out, you get dressed and then return to your newspaper, but you can't remember where it is, so you spend some time looking for it. In the meantime, you accidentally knock over a vase and it smashes. That's not good, so you head into the kitchen to get a cloth and the vacuum. You remember that you haven't washed your breakfast plates yet, so you stop to do that. All washed up now. Oh look, there's your newspaper! You put it under your arm and head out to read it.

On walking out, you step on the broken vase. Thankfully you had your shoes on by this point, so it didn't hurt, but you should really clean it up now, so you head back into the kitchen to get the cleaning equipment. Out you go to clean up the broken vase, but there's a knock at the door. It's your friend, so you stand there chatting for an hour or so, and head on back into the house to carry on reading the newspaper... I mean, cleaning up the broken vase. Anyway, you finally managed to clean up the vase, so you go ahead and do the dishes, and finish up with... ah jeez, where'd I put the mail?

I know, I know, I'm totally exaggerating, but honestly, watch carefully, and this is how people live their daily lives. This is how people attempt to run their

67

businesses. It's disorganised, and it's definitely not efficient. Of course, you have to maintain and be reactive and be proactive to make progress, correct? So, how do you do it? In a focused way. Eat, wash dishes. Shower, clean the shower sides. It's the same as write sales letter, upload sales letter. Write chapter one, plan chapter two. Get the mail, deal with the mail. Break the vase, clean the vase.

And people ask, 'Why do I feel tired? Like I've worked my fingers to the bone, yet I've barely made any progress!' This is why. Broken Vase Syndrome. Watch for it, avoid it. Spot the broken vase, clean it up immediately and you could double the amount of progress you make daily, whether it's business, or personal.

Stick with me, because next up we're getting back to the good stuff next. No task for this last tip here, aside from watch... and listen.

See you in chapter two!

> # Self-mastery and self-discipline are the foundation of good relationships with others.
>
> Stephen R. Covey

CHAPTER TWO
Having a Vision of Success
How Adequate Are Yours?

Have you seen all those entrepreneurial schools popping up all over the place, teaching the unteachable?

All us old business people that have picked up our experience through our actions, testing, tracking and generally getting things wrong in order to learn a new skill, always have these conversations about how nothing really substitutes real experience. You can't teach entrepreneurship in school, we used to say.

Well, it turns out we were wrong. I caught word that one of the most imperative attitudes to have towards your business they have begun to teach. Finally, schools and university courses are starting to bridge the gap with the real world and use their sense, instead of just being a big memory test and time sink. Good on them. It's about time.

So, what are they teaching? Simple. They're teaching how important it is to have the right attitude and good communication skills. But they have to be prepared to both learn and unlearn at the same time to move ahead of their competitors. That means they have to stop making EXCUSES and learn that by making this change, their life can and will be better. Sadly though, this is still rare, but at least it's started.

What's the first thing that pops into our mind before we even begin to build our businesses? Even before we've decided for sure that we want to go ahead and build our businesses? Let me tell you what popped into my mind before I started out. I had this vision of a website. It wasn't any ordinary website that just had integrated ad tracking, the odd bit of content or anything as dry as that. I was thinking ad tracking, auto-responders, ad reviews, website reviews, regular content updates, a thriving community, live chat, superior design; all the bells and whistles. I imagined people flocking to this site and using it as a home for their business, a base of operations. I was excited. What can I say? It might not seem like much now, but even in 2008, that was one heck of a website.

Anyway, it was always my vision of the perfect business that pushed me every day. Always dwarfing what was achieved the previous day in quality and quantity, and finally it was finished. With my marketing plan in hand, I began promoting. It was an incredible feeling.

My first customers. I did all of this myself, nobody else, just me, my mind and a plain blank sheet of paper. What an achievement, the vision of my perfect business brought into reality by my own hands.

The marketing plan went well, and before long I'd hit my 100 member mark. For the next year and a half, the site kept growing and became more a reflection of what I had in my mind as the perfect business. It was everything that my customers could ever want, at a price they were very willing to pay for such quality, plus it was making me a solid monthly income. Everything was coming alive perfectly.

After about a year and half of maintaining, updating, changing and improving, it became apparent that due to bandwidth costs, I couldn't really take the site much further. That wasn't in the original plan. Auto-responders and ad tracking became commonplace. I was competing with the best marketers out there.

These people had over a million on their lists. I, on the other hand, had only 3,431. I was still very young as far as my marketing brain was concerned. I had neither the promotion power, nor the expertise, to be able to build on what I was doing, even though I was trying as hard as I could with the budget I had. Things were getting harder as people's lists grew.

My customers were building more and more resources, it was getting more and more costly to keep them and it was cutting into my profits. Not to mention the tools I was offering became totally saturated as a million and one copycats emerged. After the initial two months, I wasn't learning or experiencing anything new anymore. I knew that I had to be making progress, not just maintaining, if I ever wanted to become one of the big guys. That would mean, however, that I'd have to totally give up my original vision and start again from scratch.

I had a million different thoughts, not to mention a bunch of my contacts, telling me different things. Keep it, you've worked hard on it, you've always said it's what you want, don't throw it all away now, and even people telling me I'd be stupid to work so hard towards something, bring a vision to life and then just walk away from it.

Then in the other ear, I had those telling me I should move on, stop maintaining and start making progress again, coming up with a new vision, moving on to bigger and better things, ditching the site altogether. According to them, I'd be stupid to try and hold on to something that wasn't working. You know what? They were right.

Even though what I had in front of me was my ideal business, it was my dream brought into reality, it represented years of work, amazing value for customers and the biggest learning platform I'd ever experienced, it just wasn't viable anymore. So, to cut a long story short, I dropped the project (after giving my customer's ample notice that I was doing so, of course). I just wasn't progressing anymore, and it was time to call it quits.

Now at the time, I knew of several others going through exactly the same thing with their sites: the endless maintenance and improvements, too proud (and maybe even worried) to give up their creation, because they'd get it to work 'eventually'. Those are the ones that told me I was making a big mistake. What happened to them?

Well, here I am six years later, and there they are, still struggling on with the same sites. No progress, just constant maintenance. Looks like I made the right decision after analysing the situation. Something I mastered a long while ago; after all, it's impossible to carry out the type of experiments I did in my diary without being able do this effectively.

I closed my first business down, much to the dismay of many of my colleagues. They saw it as a failure, as a weakness. Something I should have stuck by and kept fighting to save, even to this day. I knew better though.

> "Trust in yourself.
> Your perceptions are
> often far more accurate than
> you are willing to believe."
>
> Claudia Black

Now what I want to do is jump to some of the observations I'd made prior to this event in my diary. I was completely unaware of the business world when most of these were made, of course, and I had no idea such observations would come in so handy in the future. A lot of my studies were based around how people get what they want. I mean, how amazing would it be to be able to get what you want all the time, and know how to do it. I was looking for a repeatable pattern that I could use myself.

There were two main methods that people used that I had noted. Both of which I've tried and tested for years, both outside and within the business world. Both of them worked only some of the time. That was a little disappointing to be honest, because that makes things far less straightforward as far as finding out what this formula for success was. The two methods that people used to reach their goals, with varying successm were as follows:

The Formula for Reaching your Goals

- *Number One* – This is my favourite of the two, and I've had massive successes in situations where things looked almost hopeless and impossible. In fact, in many cases, it's gone even further and I've found myself not just winning, but far exceeding what I thought was ever possible. Constantly amazing others and myself with the rate of progress and forward movement, both personally and in business. This method was quite simple. It was pure unadulterated, stubborn determination. Always clawing for new heights. When someone said it was impossible, I'd often go and do it just to prove them wrong. Clawing at the impossible and always breaking new ground, no matter what anyone around me said. This is a big part of what's got me here today, but it's far from the ideal situation.

What I found was, that by cutting out other people's opinions and thoughts, where I'd become massively successful in many situations, in others, I'd expend unbelievable amounts of time and energy, only for it all to come to nothing. A complete blank. In addition to that, I'd be none the wiser as to why I failed, so I wasn't learning anything either. It was make or break. Outright success beyond all expectation, or complete failure.

- *Number Two* – Method number two was something that I never really liked doing. Being swayed by other people's thoughts and opinions. Changing my actions depending on the reactions of others. I'm sure you can all relate to some time in your life where you'd done something, and prevailed, and thought to yourself, 'If I'd have listened to that person telling me not to do something, I would have failed. I'm glad I didn't listen'. Ever had that?

That's why I tend to shy away from this. I still don't think it's smart to listen to what others say about your project. I used to see some people having major successes just listening to other people in my younger days, but you know what? They were only listening to people that had already trodden the path they wanted to tread. They weren't just plain old opinions and 'guesses'.

Nowadays, everyone wants to speak out and give their opinions on something when actually, they're not qualified to do so. I wouldn't write about business if I didn't have the know-how and learned the methods that took me from nothing to success. That'd be plain ignorant. The fact of the matter though, friends, family, or even random strangers, will have an opinion on what you do.

No matter how close they are to you, are they really qualified to tell you what you should and shouldn't be doing with your business? Unlikely. Are those that own their own businesses, but have yet to quit their jobs and be totally self-sufficient, qualified to teach you about business? Nope. They might have their own businesses, but if they haven't reached their goals yet, how on earth could they possibly point you in the right direction without guessing, or just stating random untested opinions? They can't.

So, out of those two methods, which one do you apply to your daily business running regime? Are you the stubborn type that just goes for what you want without any regard for other people's opinions of what you can and can't do? After all, shouldn't it be your choice what you achieve and what you don't? Or, are you on the other side of the fence?

You value other people's opinions and thoughts on what you should and shouldn't attempt, and take those into account when making important decisions. After all, they're the ones who know what you're capable of, right?

You see, I've found something. It's profoundly strange in a world where most people fit into one of the above two categories. You see, when striving for success, there's only one method that beats either of the above, and it's a little of both. That method is simple. You use method one, you drive onwards towards success, you drive hard, you push the boundaries every day in order to achieve the lifestyle you want. In addition to this, however, you listen very carefully. You listen to other people's thoughts and opinions, and you watch them, learn from them, and apply it to your actions, but (and this is a big but) you only apply this information from people who are qualified to advise you. Are they qualified to tell me what to do? Do they know all the facts? Are they experienced in this field themselves, or are they just giving out random thoughts and opinions?

This is a minor point though and isn't really what I'm putting to you here.

I want you to remove yourself from both of the above situations. From this point on, you are no longer stubborn, setting a single goal and striving until you succeed. If you do this, you will fail to adapt adequately and you will waste years of your time. It isn't the goal that's unrealistic, it's how you're trying to get there that's unrealistic. I'll explain further in a moment.

From this point on, you no longer take opinions and thoughts into account from anyone who doesn't have all the facts. Totally write off everything unless it's from someone who has trodden the path you want to tread. When you exceed and overtake those advising you in this way, you once again will write them off, because at that point they're just guessing.

How can they know what you need to do to progress when they're further behind than you are? Not possible.

> If you want to know
> what lies ahead
> on the road,
> ask someone walking
> back towards you.

Now I have to apologise in advance, because I can't very well give you the whole point of this section without first explaining the above to some extent. Some people may not be reading this whole book, and I don't want them to go changing their business about with that valuable information, because they'd just end up mad at me for not giving them the whole story. My point here is this:

What does the vision you have in your mind right now of where you want to be when your business becomes a success, look like?

What are your surroundings like? What new belongings do you have? Where do you live? What car do you drive? How much do you earn? There's absolutely no harm in imagining these things, because they're your goals. It's what you're working towards, and what you would consider to be the perfect life.

Let me put this to you though. Now I want you to imagine your perfect business. How many hours do you spend working on it daily? How many websites do you have up and running? How many employees do you have? Can you see your logos, your design, your whole image?

How about your workstation – multiple screens maybe? My point is this, and it's a big one, so listen up:

How do you know that your vision of success is possible? The end results are fine, the car, the house, the holiday homes, the belongings, but what about the process? How do you know those websites you have in mind will be able to get you to the lifestyle you're after? How do you know those products, that number of employees, that design, that style and that approach will get you to where you want to go? You don't.

See, I finally figured it out. The only time being absolutely stubborn and clawing your way to success, no matter what works, is on a large scale. 'I want that house' works. 'I'm going to buy that car' works. 'I want a business that makes a million pounds a month profit' works.

'I only want to work on my business three hours a day' doesn't work. 'I want 100 employees' doesn't work. 'I want 10 websites' doesn't work. You can only afford to be stubborn about the overall goal, the long-term. You cannot, on the other hand, be stubborn about the process, the way in which you reach those goals.

Remember back to the very first example I gave you about closing my business down and how everyone had different opinions? I knew what I wanted, I knew what my business goals were, but my idea just didn't provide the income and the viability that I needed to reach my goals. So, I changed it (much to the horror of my colleagues who couldn't understand why I wasn't being stubborn and pushing for success like they were). You already saw the result there, and how I've pushed far ahead of anyone I knew from the beginning of my career that started when I did.

Let me ask you, are you being stubborn and clawing for success, no matter what anyone says, striving to achieve your goals? Brilliant if you are. That's the only way to succeed in my experience.

Let me ask you another question

Are you directing the same attitude at the day-to-day running of your business? If so, you're making a big mistake. How do you know how to run your business in a way that will ensure you reach your goals? You don't. The only way to go is keep testing, tracking, trying new things, pushing boundaries, learning from those that have already trodden the path, and adapting. That is the key here. If you push too hard to stick to your vision of the perfect business at the process level, your business will suffer, and you'll never actually make any progress.

If the vision of your perfect business has survived intact for longer than a month, then you're doing something wrong, and it could well be this factor holding you back from success. Changing your plan doesn't mean you're a failure, it doesn't mean you've given up on your goals, but if there's one thing you have to accept here, it's that the success of your business depends on one thing. Your customers. Not you, but other people. That's hard to accept for some, I agree. Ultimately, however, you might be in control of the day-to-day running, but if no one buys from you, then you're never going to see that lifestyle.

Customers change. Fashions change, lifestyles change. Everything changes so quickly that if your business isn't changing with it, you're getting further and further behind your hopes and goals for the future, just like those people I met and who I left behind that have been messing with the same website, trying to make it their dream business since the 2008. I don't even recognise my business three months down the line, it's changed so much, never mind six years ago.

The Task For Today – Should You Choose To Accept It – Analysing your business, your goals, and the process

OK, picture me rubbing my hands together now, because that's exactly what I'm doing for reasons that shall become clear in a moment. What I'm going to ask you to do now is something that's been with me since I was in my early school years. It's something that is almost solely responsible for my success today, and will continue to be in the future. Something that from the moment you begin to make use of it, you make progress, you learn something, and things start looking up. It doesn't take years. It's just a matter of days.

Oh, you guessed it. I want you to treat yourself. Jump on the internet preferably, unless you have a John Lewis store near you. Buy yourself the biggest, smartest, cleanest most expensive diary you can find. The best craftsmanship, the best cover and the best pages. Forget accessories like calendars, refillable pages and stuff like that. Just a simple, A4 or A5, top quality journal. Whichever size suits you the best.

Go for it, why not order it now? When it arrives, treat it with respect. It's something special. Nobody touches it, but you. It's yours, and for your eyes only. A place for you to record your thoughts, but most importantly, it's a record. When things go wrong either in your business or personal life, you can look over it.

It will show you where you went wrong. When things go well, on the other hand, it'll show you what you did and how to reproduce your results. The more you give it, the more it gives back. Treat it as your most treasured possession. Something more valuable than money could ever buy.

If you're stuck for what to write as far as business is concerned, I'm going to help you get started. Write about this book, what you're reading now. Talk about what you've tried, what worked, what didn't work. Note down your opinions on what I'm saying, whether you agree or disagree. Write down notable points that you believe to be important, how to put them into action and what kind of results it gave you. Before long, you'll be off on your own tangents, writing about other things, what you learn and how you're going to use it later. Have a read-through every couple of weeks to refresh your memory.

In addition, you could (if you wanted to) begin to write about your business vision. It's important to be able to differentiate between the process and the end result. Remember I talked about the stubbornness and how it applies to one but not the other just a moment ago? Well, I guarantee if you ask someone else to describe you, your qualities, your bad habits, what you're good at and what you're bad at, they'll come up with some things that you never even realised you were doing, could do, or were good at.

Paul Wakefield

The diary is the same concept. It's like recording yourself and playing it back. 'Do I really sound like that?' You get a true picture when you can see what's going on in the third person. It's far easier to judge your next move. Try it. You won't be disappointed. You'll be the one acting on your knowledge, and what you've learned works and doesn't work. Everyone else will have no clue why they go wrong or why something goes right. Leave them to fumble in the dark. You? You, however, can switch on the light, just like that. Everything will become clear. Best of all, it'll only take you five minutes.

> "Never give up! Failure and rejection are only the first step to succeeding."
>
> Jimmy Valvano

How To Win – Even When You Fail

Without kidding yourself, self-help style!

It occurred to me a long while ago that people, no matter who they are or what they're fighting to achieve, cannot take the good with the bad. My automatic reaction to failure for as long as I can remember has been 'Oh well, no worries. That didn't go to plan, but I learned something, and there's always tomorrow'. The majority of those around me, however, don't see failure as an option. Whether they didn't get their promotion at work, or they messed something up at home, it's always a negative experience, and they beat themselves up about it and dwell on it for way too long. Sometimes months, or even years.

Paul Wakefield

There's two things I'd like to get out of the way immediately

•   Failing is a learning experience. It is not something to be dwelled upon, and to be honest, it doesn't really even matter all that much if you fail, because you gain something from the experience.

•   Secondly, taking the attitude of 'Oh well' rather than 'Failure is unacceptable!' is not a way of hiding or running away from things that have gone wrong. Even though it may seem that way to someone on the outside, when you brush off a major drawback as nothing but a minor annoyance, it's completely the opposite. The fact is, you can't change the past, you can only learn from it. We all know that, but very few of us have acted on this knowledge. When was the last time you said or thought 'I wish I did X action at Y time'?

The fact is this. Dwelling on failures and things that have gone badly in the past will only teach you something that you can use in the future. You can't change what's happened, but you can look forward. With so much hype about ignoring your past and only looking to the future, I'm shocked that anyone ever learns anything.

Looking at the past is imperative. Never listen to someone who tells you to ignore it, because it's self-defeating. You'll find yourself in limbo, making the same mistakes over and over again and making very little progress. Failing and lack of success is the most vital learning tool we have, and yet there are those out there telling you to ignore it. This disgusts me.

This section is dedicated to removing the myths about falling short, and learning how to use it to your advantage. By the end of this section, you will be embracing your shortcomings and using them in such a way that you can make progress far faster than anyone who tries to hide from them, ignore them, or falls into the positive thinking trap.

I'd just like to say at this point, that if someone came to me and said 'I only have 10 minutes. Tell me about one thing that has had the single most profound impact on your success', I would give them this section. It's a massive confidence builder.

> "No man ever became great or good except through many and great mistakes."
>
> William E. Gladstone

Paul Wakefield

How self-help made failure taboo

And scared the pants off people in the process!

Some of the more recent self-help publications worry me. I can take one look at any sales letter selling a performance enhancing book, and through their bullet points, I can tell you with confidence and 99% accuracy whether what they teach will work, will not work, or even do more damage than good. How do I know?

My diary, of course. Sure, everyone is different, but after testing my methods for so long and proving beyond a doubt they work on hundreds of occasions on myself and the people I meet, my customers and my contacts, both inside and outside of business, I can say with confidence that I'm more qualified and have probably the best set of quantifiable results in front of me right now than anyone that had a year or two of success and decided to write about it.

Which is how I can tell you right now of the devastating consequences of one my most hated points made by other so-called experts writing their performance enhancing books. Here is just one of the examples I can think of off the top of my head. We have the recent spate of positive thinking books that tell you things like 'If you think hard enough about something, it will happen'. And, 'If you only stay positive and always think about the good things, and what it'd feel like to reach your goals, it will happen'. After all, cause and effect, right? If you think about failing, you will fail. If you think about succeeding, you will succeed – at least, that's what they say.

No Excuses, No Limits

To some extent, I agree. It's not all bad. When you're feeling like you're on top of the world, it often puts you in a better position to product higher quality work. Your end results are often better, and you do reach your goals more quickly. However, if you've ever bought one of these books and tried to carry out the exercises (as have I, for my diary's sake), you'll find yourself worrying even more. I mean, what if you think a bad thought and it happens? What if you begin to attract bad things by your bad thoughts? How can I get these bad thoughts out of my head? Oh no! Bad things are coming to me now because I thought negatively. I must try and force myself to think positively or I'm in for trouble. All of these things sprung up in my mind when testing these products out. It doesn't actually help at all. In fact, it hinders. I was spending more time worrying about what I thought than making progress.

I actually have this bookmarked, and after attempting this method for a couple of weeks, I was a wreck. On condemning the absolute untested crap I was reading, I made a smarmy comment. It read, 'Next thing you know, they'll be trying to sell me another product that tells me how to control what I think about and avoid those negative thoughts. From a marketing perspective, not only is the original product very clever by teaching people they can solve all their problems by doing nothing but thinking, but then you have the fear factor to sell on to'.

You can guess what landed in my inbox a few weeks later. 'Are you attracting bad things because you can't control what you think about? Can't ignore those negative thoughts? Buy my new book quickly because you're heading for disaster!' So predictable.

87

I'll say it again. Crushing your natural thoughts, your negative feelings and your past failings will stop you from being able to see clearly whether you're moving toward or away from your goals. It hinders you from being able to make judgements in the future from your past experiences. Something that these books are teaching people to avoid is the very thing that my success has been built on.

Taking a quick glance at my diary, I can give you non-stop, almost daily situations where either mine, or someone else's success has been built on this concept.

Stick with me here, because there are important points to make about this

- **Point number one** – Those who benefit from this attitude all respond to failure in the way I mentioned earlier. 'Oh well, I'll learn from it, let's move on'. None of them dwell on the failure itself, but the lesson it taught them. To them, failing is just like success. It just doesn't bother them all that much, aside from the small tinge of disappointment.

- **Point number two** – Learning from your mistakes is a dangerous game. If you try to start up a business and fail, do you never try to start up a business again because you failed last time? No, you don't. And this is one of the only places where these bog-standard sit back self-help books do help (as much as I hate to admit it). You set a goal. You try and achieve that goal. If you fail, you don't drop the goal and decide you can't do it. Instead, you look at the process and change that.

The biggest drawback to this method is that rarely can people distinguish between process and result. What you'll find happening is that they'll attempt to reach their goals and if they don't make it, they drop their goal altogether. All is lost from that point on, because they haven't learned where to apply this technique and where it's best left alone.

Do you see now how things aren't so cut and dried? It's not about ignoring your mistakes, but it's not about dwelling on them either. It's not about having a positive mindset all the time, but it's about learning how to figure out when and where to act on your negativity, and I'll be honest with you here, I don't think that there is a happy medium; at least I haven't found it in all my years of searching and recording my findings.

Notice we're covering a lot of points very quickly now. This isn't just black and white, so I'd suggest reading through that section again, because I don't think it's all that easy to grasp the first time around (I should know, it took me 50+ times to get this right through my diary entries). This might be a good time to make use of your new diary too, if you chose to start one at the end of the last section (which I highly recommend – more highly than any advice I could give to anyone about anything).

> "Success in the end erases all the mistakes along the way."
>
> Chinese Proverb

Why not start picking out quotes and testing them for yourself? That's what I'd do if I were in your position. Just start carrying out little experiments of your own. I can confidently say, if I hadn't done this, I'd probably still be on that bench (if I was even here at all). I might sound obsessive, but when you consider it was just a few pages of A4 lined paper, a pen and 15 minutes of my time a day that showed me the path to tread to get back to my previous standard of life (and exceed it), I don't think it's all that overboard.

And now we're going to move on to something even more profound. This should have you feeling much more confident about making an attempt, because as you're about to hear, those glossy successes that people make themselves out to be aren't exactly a true representation of what's going on.

It's not just you.
It never is.
It's everyone.
And it can mean ultimate success.

Finally dispelling the myths about success... And revealing the truth about failure

This is something that I left until the middle of this book on purpose. Because those who have dismissed everything I've said so far won't have their diary, won't have tried any of this, and won't be prepared to dispel the myths about success. They just wouldn't be able to handle this part of the book. If you're still with me, I know you can at least take it on board and think about it, even if you end up totally disagreeing with everything I say, or you have your own conclusions based on previous experience.

I do have a quick little fact for you though that sets the scene for this whole section, and will make you infinitely more comfortably with this notion of failure and should give you that 'Hey, whatever!' attitude I've been raving about for the past few pages.

That fact is this: nobody I have ever met has succeeded more than they have failed, not even the most successful multi-millionaires.

I'm sure there's a few people out there that are the opposite, but they're few and far between. Let me explain with a few examples.

I've recently been learning about the property investment, and when it comes to this summer and my training is over with, I'm going to be doing this for real. Now the amount I learned from both my marketing and pre-marketing days allowed me to figure out how to learn a new skill, perfect it and exceed the teacher in a very short space of time. Thank you, diary. (That's how powerful it is; if you haven't started one yet, I'd seriously consider it. All it takes is 15 minutes per day).

I'll be talking about learning at such a pace later on in the book, but for now, it's safe to say I find someone successful, and stalk them. Well, not literally, but I go to their seminars, read all their material and watch them while they work if I get the opportunity to do so.

Now my mentor, the guy who's teaching me about property investment, has made an unbelievable amount doing what he does best. He has very similar views to myself, and his concepts of the journal or diary are also very similar, except instead of using his for everyday life, he's been using it for 15 years to master the property investment industry. This is the type of person I have total confidence in learning from.

Anyway, it might surprise you to find out, that even today, he fails more than he succeeds, yet he still makes the money where other property investors fall flat on their faces. If you're familiar with the property industry, you'll be familiar with this phrase: 'Let your profits run, and cut your losses short'. It means exactly what it says. When you buy and things go your way, you let them keep going, not ridding yourself of your equity too early, until things begin to move against you. On the other side of the coin, cutting losses short is quite simply selling early if you don't understand why something happened, or it does something you didn't expect and moves against you (rather than waiting and hoping it'll do something different). You cut it and run. It's the same with the stock market too. So I've been told, anyway.

Now the reason this guy makes so much money so quickly when he fails more than he loses is because of the above statement. The profit he makes from a successful property far exceeds the loss from unsuccessful properties.

This doesn't just apply to the property industry either, oh no. I was speaking to a good friend of mine a week or so back, and he told me that he and his contacts (all in to search engine marketing) actually lose on more keywords than they win on. One winner out of nine tries is the figure he quoted me, yet still he maintains $300-$900 per day in pure profit. How does he do it? He lets his profits run and cuts his losses short, that's how.

I want you to notice again that the failings and shortcomings are coming in the process, not the overall goal. This has been a trend throughout this book and it will continue to be so.

If you're not failing, you're not trying.

If you're not trying, you're not making progress.

If you're not learning from your past, you're making the same mistakes.

> "The one thing that separates the winners from the losers, is, winners take action."
>
> Anthony Robbins

Paul Wakefield

The task, if you wish to accept it,
Learning to accept

So, there we have it. I hope you got something out of this section. There's far more here than I could possibly wrap up into one single point or task. As you probably noticed though, there are many aspects to what I just explained to you. If you take the time to write them down, it's very probable that you'll get far more out of it than from a quick read-through.

That's it though, that's my final push to get you to start one. If you haven't ordered yourself one yet, it's very unlikely that you will. Like I say though, that's entirely your choice. Giving the power to choose back to you as a means of success is, after all, what I wanted to achieve here.

Anyway, I have a new task for you today. That task is to watch and learn to understand one thing. The first of which relates to section one of this chapter, and that's how see and learn from your failures.

This is really easy to do. All you have to do is look back at some situations where you haven't succeeded as well as you'd like. Maybe you're not getting to where you want to be right now? That's fine, not a problem. I want to dispel any fears you might have, or have had previously, about the times you haven't been able to achieve. With this, I hope you'll be able to look back and say with pride that you screwed up. Know deep down that everyone screws up, even the successful screw up more than they succeed. They just recognise when to change the process. They never give up on the overall goals.

It shouldn't make you feel bad, let down or embarrassed. Quite the opposite. You can say to yourself, I failed because I dared to try where others would cower away from such a challenge, and now I'm better equipped to succeed next time.

I think the most important thing to keep in mind here is that it doesn't affect you anymore. It might have done at the time, but you're not there any more, so it can't hurt you. It shouldn't make you feel like you did when you first made the mistakes. That let down feeling should be all but gone, because things are different now. A brand new situation, a brand new business vision, looking to achieve the same goals, but ultimately shaped by past slip-ups.

An ideal first entry for your diary (Sorry, I couldn't resist)

I don't believe thinking about past failings is self-defeating as others seem to. Not only does it let me learn and teach me new things, but it always helps me make speedy progress. I prefer to face it, take what I can from it, and then move on. It's hard to make progress unless you've dealt with past failures. This subject just shouldn't be taboo. It's never done me any harm, and I've been acting on this attitude since my business began, possibly before my business began if I'm honest.

"It's fine to celebrate success but it is more important to heed the lessons of failure."

Bill Gates

Paul Wakefield

"It's what you learn after you know it all that counts"

John Wooden

CHAPTER THREE
The Truth about Making Progress Fast
The Facts About Learning

If there's one thing I've learned in my years before and after getting in to business, it's how to learn. Learning is the underlying basis of success. You can't make progress and change the situation unless you're learning something. Unless you're changing the situation, it's impossible to reach the top in a short period of time, unless the situation happens to change in your favour (which is highly unlikely and a lot more long-term, and requires something I don't like to rely on. The actions of other people).

I know learning how to learn sounds like a strange concept, but I assure you, it's not. You see, unlike during our school years when our teachers were taught to teach, and we knew without a doubt they had all the knowledge to pass on to us, when you get into the real world, what's immediately obvious is everyone knows everything. Or they think they do.

What's actually happening is their opinions are being put forward as fact. They don't have a diary, or any past results that have been tested on hundreds, if not thousands, of people. It's just their opinion. This is why we get people trying to teach a subject they have no idea about. This doesn't apply to everyone, of course, but you can see how learning in the real world is very different from the type of learning we've been conditioned to accept from the moment we set foot inside a classroom. This is why one of my priorities has been learning how to learn.

The worst thing about this is, it's so obviously simple, yet it took me years to figure it out. What an idiot, I thought. That was until I looked around me and saw the majority of those striving for success making the same mistakes as I was. I'll be honest, when I started out in business I had no idea about anything. This isn't even something that hit my diaries until two years back, yet it's done me the world of good.

Once I'd nailed my erratic progress, sometimes winning in a matter of days at something that would take someone else months, and sometimes spending years on something that someone else does in a matter of months, it hit me, that aside from my stubborn streak (which we talked about earlier, so I won't repeat it here), the other thing that was holding me back was my inability to learn. Once I got to this stage, I began to test it.

I tested it with my own business. There are thousands of people out there losing money, struggling to move on in their business, going on gut feelings instead of facts, having inadequate rules. Some of whom I've been reading about and in fact meeting more recently, have been doing it for over 15 years! Yet I come along, I learn using my methods, and within a month, I'm seeing huge profits come from my efforts. Am I naturally talented? Yeah right, I don't have a single natural talent. Well, not actually true, but you get my point. Everything I do on a daily basis, whether it's personal or business, is something that I've learned how to do from others around me. I'm useless when I start out.

Don't get me wrong either, it wasn't always like this. When I started in business, before I'd even learned how to learn properly, it took me nearly two years and five failed websites before I figured out what I know now and put it into action. The moment I did, what happened? I started to surpass some of those who you probably haven't heard of yet in the online business niche, but I looked up to them. Three months later, my life had changed, and that was at a pretty relaxed pace doing maybe four to five hours a day, four days a week. The only thing I did differently was begin to listen to different people in different ways.

Since then, I've applied these methods to sports and hobbies that I enjoy. I mean, I've always enjoyed messing around and I've always been OK at sport, but I've never actually been as good at any of it as I knew I could of been. Until now, of course. It's great. Fun without having to lose all the time. You'd be surprised at the comments that come my way about quick progress from people who have no idea what I was doing.

"A wise man can learn more from a foolish question than a fool can learn from a wise answer."
Bruce Lee

I applied to healthy eating and cooking. I can cook up one heck of a meal now in 15-20 minutes, where previously it was just a TV dinner or instant meal. I managed to change my daily habits. I'm in better shape now than I've ever been, even my younger self wouldn't be able to compete, and of course, I have a successful business. Most of these I was terrible at. I was absolutely the worst of the worst, especially when it comes to cooking and eating healthy.

Of course, none of these things might be important to you. Everything I tested this with so far has been important to me, and what I'm about to show you can simply be applied to what you feel is important to you. It's likely going to be completely different to my list, but that's OK, that's not a problem. There's no reason why it can't work. If one of the points on your list happens to be business and, in particular, online business (which it very likely is if you got your hands on this), then great news. There's some common ground that we have. That's the very first thing I ever used this method on to great effect.

Before we move on, I want to warn you of something. What I'm about to tell you, you may have heard before. You may even know about them already, but please don't dismiss them. This would be number one on my list of steps to success at speed. Without it, it could happen, but it'll take much, much longer. Four years of hard non-stop work, compared to seven months of relaxing, don't care too much, not really all that hard work. That's the difference it made for me.

If you're keeping a diary now, then check yourself and your entries daily. You might know how, but are you putting it into action? If not, knowing how means nothing.

Whatever you do though, don't write it off. Test it out. You might well be pleasantly surprised at the results.

First things first
The art of being a stalker

OK, so maybe being a stalker is a bit over the top, but what I'm about to share with you does bear some very big similarities. OK, so first things first, one of the things I missed at the very start was to attach myself to someone who knew what they were talking about. There's some very important factors that need to be taken into account when doing this though.

The person that you attach yourself to cannot just be someone who thinks they know what they're talking about. It's everywhere nowadays; people will say and do anything to sell some products, people who don't have the first clue about ethics or business that just happen to have access to the internet. They will drag you down, waste your time and take your money for the trouble.

When I say time, I'm not just talking 10 or 15 minutes. I'm talking years of your life, tens of thousands of pounds of your money, and in severe cases, far more, all as a result of someone trying to teach something they have no idea about. An opinion sold as fact.

This is precisely why you have to be really careful about just who you choose to follow, and no matter how independent you are and like to be, this is the only way to learn quickly.

Bear with me here; I did say that you may have heard this before and have taken this into account already, but it's important that you're carrying it out, and carrying it out correctly. If you're not moving at the pace and making the progress you'd like to be making, and you are actually trying and carrying out the methods you learn, you may be learning the wrong things from the wrong person. They may not even be teaching you incorrectly on purpose.

Whichever category you fit into, already know this, or don't already know this, keep reading and we'll try and turn that slow progress around to be something a lot more... comfortable, and fast, of course.

So, let's begin with the basics, shall we? I'm going to talk in a business sense here, seeing as this is what this book is aimed at, but you can use this for anything. First things first then; when looking for role models and someone who's achieved something that you'd like to achieve, the first step to getting to know about them and how they got to where they are today, is all the free stuff. Jump on their list. Do your research. Check out customer testimonials.

One or two can be faked for sure, but out of those that I've seen that so obviously do fake such feedback, none of them ever have more than 10 or so, especially not stretched over years and multiple products. This is the first step to ensuring that their methods work. Who are others talking about? Who has the most, and the best, testimonials? Who has the business that is the most similar to your hopes and goals for the future?

Maybe you can find multiple people? Forget learning for now though. Take it at face value. Just find the people who meet your expectations, those that you can be sure are successful and make a connection. We'll leave the learning until later. Hey, you could even pick more than one if you want, but be very careful if you do. You're looking to stay focused, find a point that they have reached, somewhere you want to be also, and then try and get there.

They need to be working similar business, in similar fashions with a similar past, with similar goals. There are so many ways to be successful, not just one, but if you try and do more than one at the same time, you'll end up with contradictory information and very confused.

One thing to keep in mind is this: you may have heard this all before, but if you're not successful, you're either not taking action, or you don't know how. Most of the book is about taking action, but this section specifically is about learning how, or even better than me trying to teach a thousand different people how to be successful, learning where to find someone to teach you how without them even knowing they're doing so.

"A real decision is measured by the fact that you've taken a new action. If there's no action, you haven't truly decided."

Anthony Robbins

Paul Wakefield

People and their history, and how it affects you

The history is the one part I want to concentrate on. I wouldn't dream of teaching people how to be successful if I was born into it. I have to admit, it would have been really nice to have a wealthy family, and it's great for those who have that. It's especially great for those who (like the majority of those that I know who were born into such families) had to make their own way. Nothing was given to them for free, and they had to constantly prove themselves and work their rear ends off to make something of themselves.

I always like to pick someone with a similar history as myself when I learn something, however. After all, teaching the techniques, methods and techniques is all very well, but there's far more to it than that. I want someone who's dug themselves out of a ditch, started from nothing, and hit it big, simply because they know more than they could ever imagine. Not just how to win at business, but how to get over the personal obstacles that stand in our way on the way to success. Everyone's situation is different. Find a successful person that suits you.

No Excuses, No Limits

It's actually really easy to do, because let's face it. People love talking about themselves, especially when they can prove a point that will sell more products, showing that they haven't been handed it all on a plate.

Now, don't get me wrong here. Gaining success and holding on to it are two very different things. Just because someone has figured out how to make it and is making a bunch of money short-term, it doesn't mean that they'll be able to keep at it. I admire those who have achieved success as much as I do those who have had it all their lives, who were born into it, and who can hold on to it, or even take it a step further. When I'm done learning how to get what I want and surpassed those who have it short-term, I'm personally going to move on to those who see long-term success. Those that have had it all their lives and know how to manage it.

What would I do with fifty million pounds in my account? (That's my 13 year target, by the way, as that will make me 50 from when writing this book.) Will I make the right moves? Will I be able to hold on to it? Sure I will, but only if I learn how from those who have already done it.

Understand that this isn't just something I'm throwing at you now, and saying you should do this or you'll fail. This is something that I permanently do myself. It's always on, I'm always striving to achieve what someone else already has while carving my own unique path. The ideal time for me to tell you that everything you're reading, have read and will read in this book, I actively practise at least daily. It's not just a cheap excuse for content.

So, to sum up, find someone not only successful, but who has built up their success from a similar situation that you're in at the moment. Look closely at their history to see if you can see any of yourself in them. If you can, that's the ideal starting point.

Paul Wakefield

Does Money Really Talk?
The bits people don't like

OK, so you've got your idol, your authority, someone to look up to. Feels good, huh? It's nice to feel like you know everything, but when you select someone yourself that you know knows more than you, it's quite the humbling experience. It's not half as annoying as someone trying to announce they know more than you. I hate that. I choose who I want to look up to using the methods in this chapter. They don't choose me. Once again, the power and potential for success comes back to you.

Now comes the bit people don't like. Buying their products. Yep, no matter how much you read their sites, how much you're on their lists or gobble up their free content, you will most likely need to purchase their products. Now, I'm not saying you can't be a success without doing this, but it does bring success far faster in my experience.

It's also far less painful when you're buying from someone you've researched and that you look up to, rather than some random person and you're not quite sure if their products will be worth it. I'm always up for buying something from someone more skilled or more knowledgeable than I am. This is what I attribute my quick success in everything I do to. The difference between my online marketing learning process and my property investment learning is huge. There's just as much, if not more, to remember about the property investing, especially as far as laws are concerned – something I've always been particularly terrible with.

With my business, I jumped around the shop, trying to learn different things from different people at different times, until one day I just said 'Stop!' I ditched everyone but those few special people who I have a respect for in that they came from the same background as me, and they have achieved what I wanted to achieve. Four years of work with limited results turned into seven months of work where I managed to achieve almost all my goals for online marketing and my income in that respect (as you heard earlier).

Do I have any natural abilities that can speed up success for me so much? Nope!

This method, however, it negates that, and often people say to me, 'You must be naturally talented at...'. That's not the case at all. I had to learn it all. This is how I do it, and this is the advice I'd give to the people who mean the most to me if they expressed any interest in business.

I know, before you say it, it sucks having to pay for information. Some people out there really have a thing about all knowledge being free. If you want to know my opinion on this (note this is my opinion), I find it very easy to buy information, because I'm not just buying something that's freely available.

I'm buying into the blood, sweat, tears, effort, the time, the money and the life experience of someone else. I'm very happy to have to scrape together every last penny I have to get my hands on their knowledge. That was very much the case when I began with this method too. I skipped paying rent to buy a product from someone.

That was until I'd acted on this information, of course; after seven short months, I didn't have to scrimp and save anymore.

It's better to buy and learn, than to abstain, and declare you won't buy information on the principal that it should be free and it's not a physical product, and you can get it for free anyway (which you can, just over a period of years instead of the seconds it takes to buy a full product). Knowledge really is power in this case.

> "To know that we know what we know, and to know that we do not know what we do not know, that is true knowledge."
>
> Nicolaus Copernicus

Contradictions and problems
How to avoid them before they start

When I began in business and got more involved with online marketing, I wasn't using the knowledge that I just gave you. I had most of it, I just wasn't using it. One of the tough challenges I came up against before putting any of this into action, and something that almost stopped this from working when I did finally put it to work, was focus.

There are so many people trying to pull you in different directions. Trying to get you to buy this product, buy that product, sign up for this freebie, subscribe to get that freebie. Stop. Literally, just stop. It's got to the point now where I almost blank everything else out.

I still keep one eye on what's going on around me, watch the trends, what's hot, what's not, who's doing JVs with who, but purely in a business sense, not a learning sense. It takes some discipline to do this, simply because when you deal with marketing, they're bound to be good at releasing products and writing copy that makes you really want to buy their stuff. It's what they do. Don't feel that you're missing out though.

If you've used the information from earlier, then you'll be on the right track, and should be getting everything you need to learn your new chosen skills. Everything outside of that can be ignored. Changing one habit at a time and learning a new skill in a short period of time is hard enough as it is, without a million voices chattering different messages in your ear.

Stay focused on your chosen role models.

Your task
Should you choose to accept it

Simple, and quick. Head on back through this section if you've forgotten anything. Once you're done, pick out a few people you admire. Those that achieved what you want to achieve. Create yourself a special inbox if you're doing this in an online marketing sense, subscribe to their lists, watch and learn. In addition, buy their products and take action.

I'd like to point out also that there isn't some hidden marketing ploy here. I rarely release my thoughts and findings as I've done here. You won't see another product like this from me for at least a couple of years now, maybe longer.

Make sure to actually use the information, however. Even if you only give it a shot for a week, the moment you act on something, the whole place doesn't seem quite so confusing or contradictory anymore. You should see immediate results.

Oh, one more thing. If you've ordered yourself a diary or a journal, even if it's just for the purpose of noting down what you learn on a daily basis in the business world, and excludes your 'real life' entirely, it's going to be an invaluable tool here. You'll be able to pace yourself and keep yourself focused much more easily.

If things start to waver, even if you don't notice it immediately, you'll see it in the pages when you start to lose focus or be pulled about in a load of different directions – ultimately this makes learning something new all but impossible, so you'll want to avoid that at all costs.

And there we have it. The few very simple, very straightforward methods that you may or may not have heard before. Even if you have heard it, your diary will make sure that you do it without you even having to think about it. Cool, huh?

*Don't make more EXCUSES,
Give it a shot!*

> Writing in a journal reminds you of your goals and of your learning in life. It offers a place where you can hold a deliberate, thoughtful conversation with yourself.
>
> Robin Sharma

Paul Wakefield

"Don't wait for extraordinary opportunities. Seize common occasions and make them great. Weak men wait for opportunities; strong men make them."

Orison Swett Marden

CHAPTER FOUR
The Opportunity is There - you just need to take it

The biggest problem most business owners and indeed people come across when we try and do something different (aside from fear of the unknown) is lack of opportunity. They're unsure whether or not they're going to be able to fit into their new project or lifestyle. Will it work? Won't it? Is there space for me? Are all the spaces already taken?

I'm here to teach you today that opportunity is everywhere you look. Every person you meet, everyone you brush past in the street, wherever you go there is opportunity. You could be far closer to outright success than it seems to you right now. It only takes one person, one event, and a matter of minutes while that event takes place to change the outcome of a situation. When I met my first JV partner in 2008, for example, it only took minutes for someone to introduce us. Immediately my problems were solved.

He had the contacts and had already built a solid JV base and resources. I was just starting out, so I didn't have much to go on. I could come up with a million ideas, but all in all, it takes time to build resources. Something I've done now, but at the time, I hadn't got, and to be honest, I didn't want to wait for it. So, I took the opportunity.

His problems were solved too. He didn't like building and managing sites, messing with scripts, graphics and designing products of a technical nature. That's where I came in as I'd learn about that stuff and was happy to do it. Now, years later, I can promote just as well as he can, and he can do all the technical stuff just as well as I can. All it took was one minute, one conversation with one of my old contacts, and my whole business turned around in a matter of weeks, and so did his. I could give you a hundred examples off the top of my head where this has happened to me, probably more.

The whole point of this chapter is to show you opportunity is everywhere, and teach you to grab hold of it even when the unthinkable is happening – and that's that; you don't know what's going on.

I mean, think about it. Who knows where a conversation will lead? Who knows where a social media post, or just a simple kind act, will take you in the future? We don't, that's the whole fun of it.

Simple acts though have a profound effect on our futures, and rather than make the mistake that the majority make, you're going to be smarter than that. You won't be looking for specific opportunities. You won't say 'I want to meet someone who already has the skills I'm lacking who needs my skills, and we're going to set off and create a successful business'. I mean, where would you find someone like that?

The best thing about this method is that you don't have to go out looking. They're coming to you all the time. Every conversation, every time you meet someone, do someone a favour; introduce one person to another (whether it's inside or outside the business world). Every e-mail you send, every single person you speak to on the phone, no matter if you know them or not. The secret to this is not looking for the end result, but setting the process in motion.

> *Recognising opportunity is about opening the doors rather than finding a pot of gold at the end of a tunnel.*

See what I'm getting at?

Let's take a look at how those around me view opportunity, for example's sake (this is my favourite subject by the way, because to this day, from my lowest point in life, to my highest, it has never ever failed me). In my diary, I noted how people, when stepping into the unknown, look for an opening for themselves. For example, starting a business. Lots of my good friends decided to start businesses after seeing me hit success. The first thing they try and do is visualise what their business is going to look like in the future. The hours they'll be working, who they'll be working with, who they'll be selling products to, how much they'll be making and so on. Recognise that from the previous section?

The whole process, however, has to be looser. Open it up, let other things happen that weren't necessarily in your plan, because it could lead far further than you originally thought. OK, now I don't want anyone to get the wrong idea and head on out releasing products all over the place without some research first, unique selling points and the like; that would be suicidal (from a business point of view, anyway). Yes, do plan, but make sure your plans are liquid and adaptable. They could change at a moment's notice and still work.

Why do most people miss opportunity? Simple, because it doesn't fit into the vision of their business, the plan they have for the process of reaching their goals, so they put it on the back burner. They get rid of it totally because it's not what they had in mind originally. This is also business suicide. As I said before, things change, and things change quickly. It's up to you to adapt your plans and take on board new developments. The goal of being rich, having spare time, getting that house or that car never changes, but the road you're going to be treading, the journey you're going to take should be totally unrecognisable from your original thought. If it's not, something is very wrong, and you've blocked opportunity out somewhere.

> "To hell with circumstances; I create opportunities."
>
> Bruce Lee

Six Degrees of Separation
The theory

OK, here's how this theory goes. If you haven't heard about it before, let me explain. It's called the six degrees of separation. It states that every person in the world is connected by no more than six links. Technically, this would mean you could go from you, to a friend, to a friend, to a friend, to a friend, to a friend ending on anywhere in the world, no matter how famous, how remote and how far away it might seem. Of course it's just a theory, but it's a very convincing one. It wouldn't surprise me at all if it was totally true, although six does seem too few. Ten, I could handle, but still, even that's very few links to go through considering you could reach anyone in the whole world (in theory, anyway).

So, exploring the theory that took my interest, I began reading books and watching documentaries about it where experiments have been carried out to see if this six degrees is possible or not.

The most notable one that sticks in my mind is a British one. They took some random guy from in London, and through only six connections, they tried to reach this hermit goat farmer that lived in the mountains of some far-off country. Two completely different people who have come from completely different backgrounds, different countries, different everything. Totally unrelated.

Anyway, to cut a long story short, after a lot of work, they managed to make the connection in just seven jumps. Not quite the six degrees, but it just goes to show how close opportunity could be. Next time you feel like things are going nowhere, have a think about this, because it always spurs me on knowing this.

> Think about it, where's your next business partner?
> Is it going to be the person you just talked to?
> Or is it going to be someone they know?
> Hey, maybe it's someone that they know,
> that their friend knows,
> that their friend knows,
> that their friend knows.

Sound unlikely? Well let me remind you that word of mouth is the most effective marketing method out there. While you're laying in bed, your friend could be talking to his friend about you, who then tells another friend about the conversation he or she had about you. Once that happens, it's easy enough to trace the line back to you if something of interest comes up in conversation.

In fact, there's actually a new age of successful CEOs coming to the surface that use this theory as a base for their business. Watch out for more news about that in business publications in the coming months and years.

Of course, there is a catch, and that catch is you have to put yourself around and make an effort, not to get an end result, but to open those doors that may produce the end result for you, or even something better. I have never have used this method and not been surprised about how fast word travels. You also have to do your bit to keep the ball rolling. Many will do it without even noticing, but the more you push it and spread the word, the more will come back to you, because there's more people out there to be talking about you in different situations. Here's two examples for you of how things work in the background without you even noticing; one that helped me, and one that I forced on purpose to help two other people. It's kind of hard to choose to be honest because there's so many situations that this has worked. I'll go for the business relevant ones for now.

Situation number one

Here's what happened to me. I joined a marketing website and made some posts on a forum, just generally joining in. The site then closed down, and I carried on with my business. Nine months later, I met a JV partner and we done well by plugging the gaps in each other's weaknesses. A complete turn around for both of us. We weren't poor, but we sure weren't doing this well. I'm pretty sure our joint projects have taken over a quarter of a million pounds this year.

That's not what really happened though. Here's what really happened. I joined a marketing site and made some posts on a forum, generally just joining in on day-to-day conversations. I made contact with a few people, and a group of us became known as 'those that know what they're talking about', even if it was early in our careers.

Before the site shut down, I introduced one of the members to another member. Two other members introduced me to another two members.

Two joint ventures came of that; one failed miserably, and one didn't go very well. It's at this point I broke out of my 'crap at marketing' stage and began building my first fully fledged site. Unbeknownst to me, one of my contacts was talking about me to someone else. Consequently we met just because my contact was using this method of putting other people's names around, or forcing the situation as I mentioned earlier.

Through this new contact's friend came a call from another marketer to put a site together. He was too busy, so he introduced us and suggested that we get together and do the site instead. This is where I met my JV partner. That's the whole story.

See how much was going on in the background there?

I guess you could call it networking, but I'm not going to call it that for two reasons. Number one is that networking is cliché and no one will ever remember this if I do, and secondly, because each one of these people in this example were doing something very important. Nobody asked to be introduced to anyone, but by one of two methods, they were talked about and got their name around by word of mouth.

The first method is just by talking to people about your current situation. Have you ever been in a situation where you've told someone, for example, you're starting a business, or you're buying a house, or you're buying a particular car, joining a club, taking up a sport or whatever. A friend, family, or colleague, it doesn't matter, but the reply comes back something very similar to 'Oh, I know someone who is doing that too!' or 'You remember you met/I told you about John the other day? Well, he's doing that too!'

It happens all the time. People don't even need to know this is the kind of reaction you're after. Tell them what you're doing and it's almost inevitable they'll tell their friends, family and contacts about you if someone they know happens to be doing the same as you are. Don't worry about people not telling anyone else about you. You and me both know they will, just because I think everyone has experienced that 'I know someone who is too!' comment from above. You don't actually have to do anything aside from talk about yourself to other people.

Situation number two

Number two is for those who know about this already, and have set out to make contacts in this way. You see, most people who declare themselves to be in networking forget one important thing. It's not a one-way street. You can't expect to be introduced to people and have new opportunities arise for you from situations you don't know that aren't even taking place, if you don't do the same for everyone else that you can. This is method two, forcing the situation to happen. Starting the ball rolling. Here's an example of how I had a hand in starting the ball rolling yesterday (yes, literally just yesterday, I do this non-stop because the results I get are so immense, it's not even funny).

So, here I was, sitting at my computer. A good friend of mine happened to be starting up a business. Naturally I was glad for him to even be brave enough to try something that's so out of the ordinary, especially at such a young age. Anyway, he's good with logos and had just got his site up and running a couple week or so ago. Up comes a message from another of my friends, and out of the blue, she has decided she wants to start a jewellery business online, but guess what she needs? You guessed it, a logo. 'Hold on a second,' I said, 'I know someone who does those. I'm sure he can sort you something out,' so I forced the situation on purpose, knowing full well that at the very least, one would be able to help the other. I put them in contact with each other.

Now bear in mind it wasn't just dumb luck that I knew someone with a logo business. Because I force the situation non-stop like this, and bring others together, it could have been someone wanting a site designed, programming done, someone good at JVs but no idea about product creation, someone good at product creation but no idea about promotion, someone with a site to sell but no promotion material, someone who has promotion material but is looking for a new project; it doesn't matter, I could have put them in contact simply because after just a few months of doing this, you'll find you have a diverse list of people with strengths and weaknesses. All you're doing is playing the matchmaker.

Anyway, I put these two in contact, and one wanted a logo, but another had nothing to give in return, and due to the budget (considering she actually has to buy stock), she couldn't pay. It's at this point most people would have stepped away and not wasted their time as they see it. I, on the other hand, stepped in and said to the logo guys; 'Look, you're new to business. I'll give you thirty minutes of consultation if you do her a logo, and then you owe me'. I had some free time anyway, may as well.

> "In sales, a referral is the key to the door of resistance."
>
> Bo Bennett

No Excuses, No Limits

Three hours later, one business owner has a logo and a new contact that makes such graphics. The logo guy now has a clue about marketing, and lo and behold, the logo guy knows someone else getting in to online business and recommended me. Not only a new contact, but a half-price consultation fee for thirty minutes at £312.50 (standard rate £625) as a favour to the logo guy, who promised me logos for my three main sites in return. Not bad for four or five hours of sitting at my computer.

Don't worry if you didn't get all that. What actually happens behind the scenes is far more complicated than what one person sees. What's important is you can see how talking about your situation and forcing the situation gives you so much potential. The next person who messages you could well have come through a big chain of people to finally reach you, and you might well go on to make millions in a really profitable business partnership. You might be able to exchange skills in any number of ways. I'm sure there's millions, if not billions, of combinations of people out there looking for other people to plug their weaknesses. Don't think it has to happen just for business either. Your next instant message could be from your future husband or wife that you met through a chain of people, it could be literally anyone or anything.

Look, I'll be honest, all you have to understand here is how to spot opportunity and make it happen for other people. When you force the situation (making it happen for other people), it will turn right back around and come back to you in the form of a new opportunity. A new method to integrate into the vision of your perfect business, saving you years of time, millions of pounds (or making you millions). And if it doesn't come right back to you in any noticeable form, then what you'll find is that others where you haven't forced the situation (used method one and just talked about yourself) will do.

Bear in mind also, that it won't happen straightaway in some cases. I've had those that I've introduced others to come back to me three years later and return the favour just by meeting someone who would fit in well with me, either having something in common, or looking to fill weaknesses with someone else's strengths.

Don't be downhearted about the time it takes though. The following get you buzzing. When I first discovered forcing the situation in 2009 and put it into action, after just three months I had 173 active people on my private messenger list from the three I began with three months earlier. Now these aren't just people I've put on my list to make it look like I have loads of contacts, these are real people. I could tell you what they all like for breakfast, what their full names are, where they grew up, what they do for a job or a business, what they do to relax, the names of their husbands and wives, what they do for a living, where they live, and more. No chat rooms or stuff like that, just two people I met in a business forum that shared similar interests, and one website owner, each introducing each other to people on a similar path.

What if those 173 people only knew 10 people?

That's almost 2,000 new opportunities for me to take. One could come to nothing, the next could make a million. If I mention something to one of them, word will get around not just to others on the list, but to others not on the list that they know. It will grow and grow, the more forcing the situation I do.

What's even better is it grows to suit your needs as well. If you're in business, and that's what you tell people, that's what they'll talk about, and more business will come your way.

If there's one thing I want you to understand here over anything, even if you only passively search for opportunity and don't force the situation to speed things up, it's that opportunity is everywhere. People just do not recognise it because the end result isn't something tangible or solid. It's not something they can put their finger on. That lack of control isn't a very nice feeling, especially if you're in business. If you want to succeed, however, you have to open the doors and then let other people come through, rather than searching for someone who's specifically going to partner with you and make both of you very rich indeed.

Of course, there's a catch. Isn't there always? This doesn't work if you rely on someone else to make you rich or achieve your goals for you. That's not how it works. Every opportunity you come across will change your plan, your approach, and the road you take to your overall goal. Most often, it'll make things easier, cheaper, and much quicker, but if you haven't started towards your overall goal yet, then you just won't be able to take these opportunities when they arise. That's if you even see them as opportunities. Use them when they come along, but don't rely on these opportunities to make you rich. You'll only get rich and reach your goals if you take them.

So, you spoke to someone about your business yesterday, right? I wonder, who will they take that information to, and who will their friend's friend's friend's friend hook you up with next? What will be the opportunity? What will be the outcome? It doesn't matter really, it can only be good if you spotted it in the first place.

You're doing better than at least 99% of the business population.

Paul Wakefield

"Take care
of your body.
It's the
only place
you have
to live."

Jim Rohn

CHAPTER FIVE
Health as a Means of Efficiency
Treat Yourself Right To Keep Your Work Up To Superior Standards

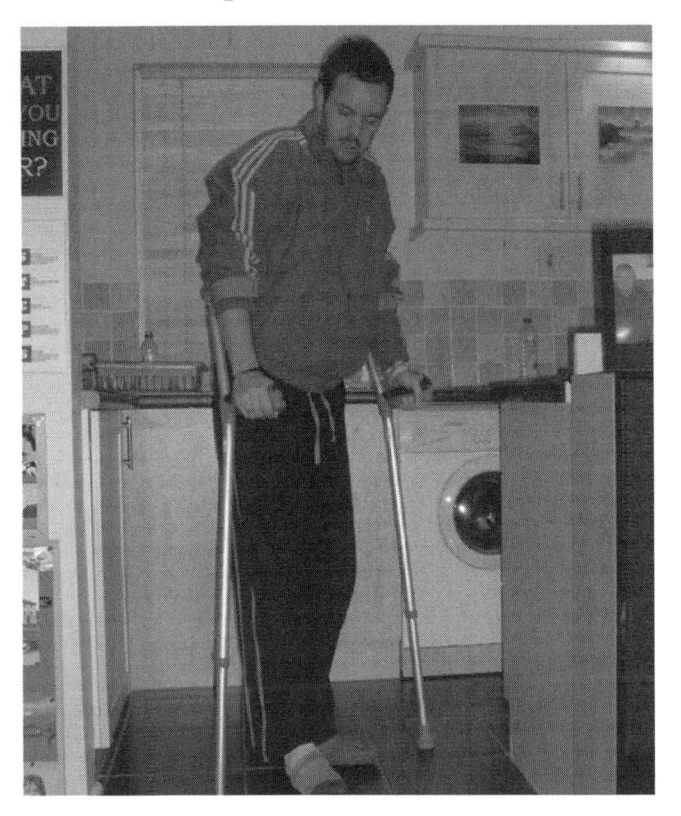

I have to admit, I rarely talk about health aspects in my business books, products or services, probably because it's a hard subject to write about when most of the people I'm writing to won't listen to reason when it comes to putting themselves before making that first million. I'm going to hope that because the structure of this book is so different, that someone out there will take note and make some big changes for the better.

I'm going to steam through this section, because everything is pretty straightforward. There's no really complicated situations that may arise, no contradictory information or long-term goals and habit forming as in the other sections. It's all stuff you can do right now. Literally, walk out the door, and come back half an hour later having completed the section.

Oh, one more thing before we get started too. Consider this another one of those dastardly disclaimers. I am in no way qualified to be giving out physical advice of any sort, as you can see from the picture. I am not a doctor or trained in the medical profession in any way. What you're about to read is my personal experiences only. Please consult a professional before implementing anything in this book related to mental or physical health.

Ta-da! That should do it. So, let's get started.

> "Physical fitness is not only one of the most important keys to a healthy body, it is the basis of dynamic and creative intellectual activity."
>
> John F. Kennedy

Mental and Physical Strains are Far Too Common

What To Expect When Learning A New Skill

Take a look at what's going on around you. This whole book is packed with non-stop, point after point methods and techniques to improve your business, your lifestyle, or the ease in which you can carry out your work with a view to reaching your goals for the future. It's all about learning.

You see, what we've got ourselves into here isn't what we experienced in schools and colleges. We're not simply remembering formulae, numbers and bits of books and publications only to recite them later and be marked on what we remember. It's far more complicated than that. What we all do on a daily basis is assimilate information and try to change our habits, integrate new timetables, and in some cases, even enhance parts of our personalities. We're judged on our actions, not what we remember, and the results are seen not on paper, but in our lives.

This is why my first healthy tip for you is something that I've been doing since I first picked up my diary. You know, with each page, even though there were many thoughts on each one, I only ever carried out one experiment at a time and attempted to learn one new skill at a time, and integrate it into my daily routine and my personality.

One thing at a time

I know you're probably really eager to succeed at multiple things, and I don't blame you, but learning more than one thing at a time can be both physically and mentally draining at times.

Changing habits and thoughts that have been with you for years is no easy task. It's tough. It's as complex and confusing enough as it is without having more than one change clash with each other, or something else to distract you where you may lose all progress through one small slip-up.

So, here's the deal. Don't try and change your exercise regime, your diet, quit smoking, lose weight, be successful in social media marketing, be successful with JV marketing, start an offline business, juggle a family life and strive for that promotion, all at the same time. Pick one and begin with that. You'll find that it's actually much faster to do one at a time than it is to do all at once, simply because your results are far more productive, focused, easy to remember and simple to assimilate. Oh, and don't think that the best way to do this is to pick the one that's the most important to you right now either. We gotta be smarter than that.

Instead, pick the one that's going to help you do the other things on your list the easiest. For example, my list went a little bit like this. I want to quit smoking, I want to lose weight, I want to be successful in business, I want to travel the world, I want to get into the property market, I want to change my diet to something more healthy. Bear in mind every one of the above is just learning about something, and that's it. It's all about changing habits, which is no easy task. I'm sure yours will be similar in nature too.

I'd say the most important to me is that I want to travel the world. So much to see, so little time, yet if I'd tried to travel the world before I made a success of my business, what would happen? Well, I either wouldn't get very far, or it wouldn't be the most comfortable trip. So, even though it was the most important to me, it would have been stupid to do that first. Instead, my list went a little like this:

Quit smoking, lose the weight to gain the confidence to be successful in life and business, get successful in business and earn enough to double my success and speed up the process by investing, then quit smoking when I could afford to take a break from one of them for just a moment and not have to worry about anything else in the world (if anyone reading has ever smoked, you'll know how annoying it is to quit when every little thing that doesn't go your way makes you want to light up, so I thought I'd get rid of those annoying things first), and then with the extra money and free time, added comfort and lifestyle additions, treat myself to a change in diet to 100% fresh, organic food. At least then I won't be eating the same food as I was when I was smoking and won't have urges to smoke after eating as badly. It worked last time…

…and just so you know, I gave up smoking in 2003.

Anyway, enough about me, I'm sure you get the picture. Plan out your future, set deadlines and target dates if you really want to do so, but don't try to take on more than one big learning experience at once. We don't quite have it as easy as our kids. This is a very different learning process indeed. Pace yourself. You're in for some hard times, and some easy times. Use the easy to prepare for the hard and not only will you get through it, but you'll learn along the way.

Paul Wakefield

Is Your Comfort Really So Important?

How To Improve Your Lifestyle In One Hour

So, why are you in business? To make a bunch of money, I'd guess. How about to improve your lifestyle too? Have more free time, maybe? That's great, me too. But the catch is, if we want free time and piles of money later, we have to put the work and some money down now. That's the price we pay for a better future. A rougher present.

You can look on the bright side though. You'll likely get back a lot more than you spend, both in free time and money. That comes later, however. If you want to get there, now is the time to take steps to make sure your journey is an easy and enjoyable one.

Time to go shopping! Hey, you may as well treat yourself, you know. No point in getting rich if you're too sick to be able to enjoy it. This is serious stuff. You want that free time in the future, you got to look after yourself now. The first order of the day is the most expensive, and probably the hardest to negotiate if you happen to be married or living with limited space or a budget. Head on out, and grab a flat screen monitor.

If you have an old computer at the moment, there's no way on earth you can stare at that thing without getting headaches, twinges, eye ache, eye strain and more. All that squinting makes me shiver. A flat screen monitor should fix all that though; my recommendation would be to get a 21.5" Mac, plus they're not all that expensive now, and you get to save some precious space if you're limited, not to mention they look neater.

No Excuses, No Limits

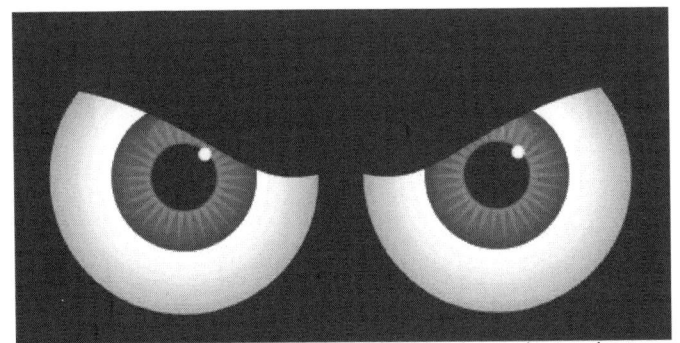

Your eyes are the most important though. I had no choice but to get mine since my hours staring at one of these extended dramatically when I quit my job. Burning eyes in the morning were not very nice at all. All gone with a flat screen now though, so grab one now if you can. If you can't, I'd make it the first lifestyle improvement on my list. 'Number One', it would read, 'Make work more comfortable'.

There's more, though it doesn't all have to be quite so expensive if you don't have the budget right now. Wrist supports, for one. A little idea I had a while ago that scarily paid off. All I did was grabbed some of those soft cloth or plastic composite material wrist wraps from a sports site on the net. They're not splints, they're not tight, and they don't restrict movement. All they do is increase circulation, warm and heal the wrist area after a long stint of work. I always wear them for a few hours after typing. During typing can restrict movement and make things worse, so that's out. Sleeping with them on is bad too, because if you're anything like me, you'll wake up in the night having fallen asleep on it and cut off the blood to one of your now cold, numb and floppy hands.

All I have to say about this is I used to get twinges and annoying pains in my wrists either during the night or just a few hours after typing. Not anymore. These warming things I wrap around my arm did the trick. Best of all, instead of £999 like the Mac, it can be done for £25 for a pair. Probably less if you shop around a bit.

133

OK, one more thing that I can't stress enough. Pretty much everything else is optional, but if there's three things that are imperative to protect from problems when working online, it's your wrists, your eyes (which we've already discussed) and, finally, your back. Oh yes, not forgetting the most common work at home ailment of all from those I've spoken to.

If you're sitting there reading this right now, perched on a wooden chair, or an over the top sofa, stop for a moment. How does your back feel? How about later in the day when you come to sleep? Are you creaking or feeling like you're going to catch a nerve every time you bend down to pick something up?

Well, don't worry. It might not be just the bones wearing down at all. I know the usual excuses: 'I'm getting old, and I feel it,' I used to say, my back creaking every time I did anything remotely strenuous. 'Time has got me'. That was until I went out and bought myself the nicest, most comfortable chair I've ever sat in.

I was broke at the time when I did this too, but I couldn't resist. Three weeks later, the only thing creaking was the chair. Turns out my joints weren't protesting at my age after all. They were protesting against my position when using the computer.

If I could advise anyone in the world who wants to be successful to buy one thing, it wouldn't be a guide, it wouldn't be a course, it wouldn't be a seminar. It'd be a huge, soft, forgiving, all day use, well-ventilated, executive chair. I ate peas and gravy for my daily meal every day for two weeks to be able to afford that. You don't want the details, but I tell you, it was more than worth it.

Treat yourself. You deserve it if you've reached this far through the book. We're coming up to three-quarters finished if you didn't see that yet, and we've been through a lot. I'll save the reminiscing for the summary though. For now, I want to move on and talk about the magic Z's.

> # "If it's the right chair, it doesn't take too long to get comfortable in it."
>
> ## Robert De Niro

Paul Wakefield

People Always Take This For Granted...
Taking Sleep Seriously
Part 1

It's something a lot of people disregard nowadays. I'm one to talk, with my longest stint ever sat in front of the computer working on my business being three and a half days straight. I'm shocked my heart didn't explode now I think about it, but hey, it was the early days, almost seven years ago now, and I was naïve. It's well known that at least eight hours out of every 24 is recommended for sleep, but hey, that's different for everyone, take more if you need more. Apparently it's supposed to go down as you get older too, but for me, it's going up. I have no problem with that though.

It's likely that if you're a smoker, or have any health problems, you may need even longer than that. Either way, it doesn't change the fact that if you suffer from lack of sleep, your business and your life will suffer at the same time. Quality will go down and so will your speed and efficiency.

This didn't actually become all that apparent until I began testing this some years ago. As a result of those tests, I stopped my ridiculous health damaging nights awake and now sleep when I feel tired. Simple as that.

I felt like I was getting much more done and had that feeling of 'everyone else is sleeping, yet I'm awake and getting a bunch of work done. I'll be massively ahead by the time they wake up.' It didn't work out like that. I would have never have known this if I didn't keep my diary. I may have had an inkling, but just how much more efficient I was being after sleep wasn't immediately apparent.

It turns out that not only was I getting almost three times the work done after sleep compared to not sleeping (300% efficiency after a good night's sleep) but what's more, after tracking my progress, I found that I was working half of the next day correcting and improving the work I'd done the previous day. I know it might sound obvious that you'd get more done more quickly after a good night's sleep, but almost four times the amount? Astounding.

Why suffer yourself, and let your work suffer, when you could be relaxing in a nice warm, comfortable bed, getting up earlier than normal, finishing your work to a much higher standard, much more quickly with much less effort.

You are trying to improve your lifestyle, not make it harder, right?

> "From reading too much, and sleeping too little, his brain dried up on him and he lost his judgment."
>
> Miguel de Cervantes

Paul Wakefield

Taking Sleep Seriously
Part 2

OK, wanting to sleep and being able to sleep are two very different things. Saying this to anyone else who works just a normal job, I'd expect them to go and see an expert, because they could have a big problem on their hands. Us home workers, however, are slightly different. It's often quick and easy to get to the root of the problem and fix it.

I remember when I first started out in business. I started to find it harder and harder to sleep, even though I was expending much more energy during the day. All sorts of things were happening. I was solving business problems in my mind while I was supposed to be sleeping, I was still coming up with new ideas while I was supposed to be sleeping (which still happens to an extent), I was coming up with site designs, site names, domains to buy, phrases for my sales letter, things I wanted to check out, publications I wanted to read, and much more.

It got to the point where I could tell I wasn't getting the sleep that I needed. I was waking up tired, started snapping at people around me, making stupid mistakes, and even went as far as having trouble remembering what I had for breakfast just an hour ago. I'm sure I looked like crap too. When I finally realised I had a problem, it took a mere week to figure out what was wrong and fix it. Almost a year of work had already been wasted though, so I'm telling you this now, so you won't waste that year.

Never work within an hour of going to bed or you'll have so many things steaming through your mind, you won't be able to relax. Speaking of relaxing, that's what you should use your hour for.

Listen to some music, watch some TV, read a relaxing book, have a shower, or just sit in silence and meditate. Whatever tickles your fancy. You could even grab some non-sugary, slow release energy food before you go to bed too. That's been proven to help sleep for a pile of reasons. (Oh and the whole myth about eating before you sleep making you put on weight is just that, a myth. Just in case you were worried about that. Calories are calories, whenever you eat. Get this right, and you'll have much more energy to work off any damage done the night before the next day.)

The ultimate trade-off.

> "Every closed eye is not sleeping, and every open eye is not seeing."
>
> Bill Cosby

Paul Wakefield

Taking Sleep Seriously
Part 3, the final part

Well I figured because it's probably the most important part of this section, I'd give you some more techniques that I use to get a good night's sleep. You'd be surprised, you know. All those people out there that still have a full-time job and don't really know what it takes to start a business are always talking about how cool it would be to branch out on their own. 'It'd be easy,' they all say to me (literally all of them).' I'd just laze about and do whatever I like whenever I like. I don't know what the problem is with all these people that find it stressful and hard work. I wouldn't.'

Well, I'm afraid those that haven't tried don't know what we know, and that's that; the transition from working for someone else to working for yourself is far from an easy one, under even the best circumstances. You've got the big potential for income and lifestyle, of course, but you're missing the security at the start, and that's not always easy to deal with.

In addition to that, when you walk out of your job and tell your boss where to go, you'll find yourself in a strange place. Suddenly work and play are fused under the same roof. They're not separate worlds anymore. Instead, they come into close proximity. Very close.

Here's a couple of methods that really helped me when I made the transition.

First, I never, ever work in bed. I tried this before, and even though it might be comfortable, in a strange way I could feel my mind beginning to associate laying on my bed with work, and it got harder and harder to sleep. Thankfully that one is easily sorted out, and my advice to you would be to avoid working in, on or around your bed at all costs. Beds are for sleeping – don't confuse the heck out of your mind if you want to continue getting a good night's sleep. If you're having problems nodding off, maybe this could be one of the problems? If not, it could well be this...

Get those darn computers, files and work related stuff right out of your bedroom. It has the same effect as working in bed. Your bedroom suddenly becomes a place of work instead of for relaxing, escaping and sleeping. Secondly, get those computers and all related equipment out of your recreation area. When you relax, you need to relax, wind down, and recharge your batteries, not have to stare at computer equipment, interrupting your mind every couple of minutes with thoughts and ideas. Save that for tomorrow or later.

This might be a good time to try and persuade your family that you need to turn that spare room into a study, if you're lucky enough to have one. If it's for your health and the success of your business, they'll understand. If you have a study already, great news! But be sure to get out of it when you go to kick back and relax after a hard day's work.

There we have it. Sleep when you need to sleep, relax when you need to relax and work when you want to work. Don't mix the three, or you'll likely get very confused, whether it's conscious or not. Those that have never had a stab at this whole business thing don't understand that this is not an easy thing to adapt to. Your whole life can change, in literally an instant, requiring new knowledge, new habits and new approaches to deal with the new situations that arise.

Separating work and play is one of those situations.

The easiest task…Ever

Yep, you're going to love this one. If you choose to accept this task, you could literally change your whole life in an hour. I'm not kidding. More energy, less grouchy, better work, more comfortable, better health and much more. If that's not changing your whole life, I don't know what is.

OK, here it is, the bombshell. Your task for today is to go shopping and purchase at least one of these off the following list. The diary that you may or may not have grabbed previously doesn't count either, but feel free to grab one of these while you're ordering too. From the least expensive to the most expensive. Loose wrist supports. One size too big for your wrists, not the splint type, to be worn an hour to two hours after typing only. Second, if you have an old computer/monitor, throw it out.

Get yourself a nice new space saving, eye saving, comfortable flat screen monitor or if you can, invest in a Mac. You'll be able to stare in it for 10 hours and your eyes will still feel better than two hours. (Breaks every hour are recommended.)

Finally, and my favourite of all - live on peas and gravy if you have to - the biggest, most comfortable, arm rested, high backed, cushioned by inflated or all day material, executive chair.

Absolute bliss.
Don't make EXCUSES!!

Which one do you need the most? Could you order it right now?

Anyway, whatever you decide with this task, remember to go see a doctor if you want professional qualified advice, or you feel something is up.

Secondly, and most importantly, looking after yourself should be a priority. It should be enjoyable, and not feel like a chore.

What's the point in being rich if you make yourself too sick along the way to enjoy the lifestyle you earn?

Paul Wakefield

"We want the facts to fit the preconceptions. When they don't it is easier to ignore the facts than to change the preconceptions."

Jessamyn West

CHAPTER SIX
Personal Perception

What People Think

Well here we are in the penultimate section of the book. Only a big old summary left after this. I'm going to miss it for sure, seeing as I've enjoyed writing it immensely. I hope you've enjoyed reading it and trying out the methods too, especially the diary bits if you've started your own.

Before we say our goodbyes though, I wanted to talk to you about one more topic, something you're inevitably going to come across if you put into action everything we've discussed here, no matter your preconceptions – and that's what happens when you become a success.

Again, because this is a business orientated book, I want to concentrate solely on money. What happens to you, and those around you, when you start reaping the rewards, and receiving the well earned gains from your efforts.

Change scares most people. At the very least it makes them a little nervous. I was no exception, even when the situation is changing for the better. Through that experience and some of the most recent significant discoveries that I recorded in my diary, I want to let you in on a few things that should put your mind at rest, and some warnings about what's going to happen, what's fact about success, what's myth, what will change, and what will stay the same. Call it your chance to see into a probable future.

First, A Warning About What Others Want To Know

What better place to start than the most important part of all this. See this book? You know all the methods you've been learning from my experiences? You know that diary that you've been keeping, allowing you to constantly improve your situations by looking at what you do right and wrong from a third person perspective? That's all brilliant, and is likely to shove you into the limelight as far as success is concerned, but why are you doing it all?

There's probably a million different answers to this question, or 500 at least. I'll keep it simple with the reason you're doing all of this is because you want to improve your business, and in turn, give yourself and those you care about a more comfortable lifestyle with all the time and money that it brings. My guess is it'll be something along the same lines for everyone reading on such a general scale.

My first warning for you is this. No matter how rich you get, you won't know it all. Our brains would explode if we knew everything there was to know about everything. Don't feel that you have to either. If someone asks you a question, think carefully before answering or giving out advice.

Do you really know the answer? Or does your newfound extra confidence that has come about as a result of your business success taken control, and you're not 100% sure, but you're pretty sure? Make sure it's the first one. Never try to teach anything to anyone if you don't have something solid to teach them.

Whether it's your friends, your family, your customers and even complete strangers, give out incorrect information and it will come back to haunt you. I know something a lot of you will be doing after completing this book, probably without even noticing it, is pointing out during conversations whether you're stating a fact, or just your opinion. Something I've done non-stop throughout this book. It has served me very well indeed over a number of years in many situations.

To be honest though, that's not really what I wanted to talk to you about. That's just the beginning. My main reason for writing these few pages here relates back to that question we answered a moment ago. Why are you here? Because you want to improve your prospects, right? That's great, but bear in mind this most important point – not everyone wants to do this.

Whatever the reason, maybe they don't care about money and material things, although I can never see how that excuse works seeing as money will allow them to stay healthy and comfortable, enjoy life to the max and probably live longer; it's always the broke people that come up with those money sayings. Harsh and totally unfair, but true.

A bit like those that despise others that are successful, just because they have money or are good at what they do. You'll never catch me giving anything but respect to those who achieve their dreams, because I understand what it means and how much it takes to get there, and keep it (which can be just as hard) and you know it too. Of course you do, otherwise you wouldn't be here right now. You'd be settling for a job and a 'normal' life and wouldn't have even tried. You've experienced and currently understand far more than you realise, many things you won't even notice until you're successful.

Anyway, before I go too far off the subject, I want to make my point. Just because you can see how you can earn a fuller and more enjoyable, more free and fun lifestyle by starting your own business and striving for success, it doesn't mean that other people understand this. Most are too lazy or scared to even try. Some don't even think that there could be a better way than £12 an hour, and others, well I'm sure they have their reasons. Whatever they are, you'll have to tread carefully.

Don't force your point on to them. You're here reading this, looking to learn to be successful because you're ready. The only person that can decide that you are ready is you. That goes for everyone else too. When you turn up in your new car, with your new house, or your new equipment and start preaching to people, or trying to get them involved, they may end up taking it the wrong way. Before you know it, you'll be cocky, you'll be up yourself, you'll be a know it all, you'll be boasting (according to them anyway). All you were doing was trying to help, but that's not how it works.

The general rule is this: if someone asks for help, you give it to them. If they don't, you don't, because it'll only backfire. They have to decide when they want to be successful. If they're not ready, there's nothing you can do.

Hey, you know, another point I'd like to make here before moving on to a word about your work hours, is that success will not change you as a person if you don't let it. Your diary will help you see any changes coming if they do happen to crop up, but as long as you keep your eyes wide open, you'll spot any glitches and correct them quickly and easily.

In addition to that, you hear this attitude that comes from me when I write? Especially when I'm ripping it out of other people's methods and the myths and general rubbish that people put out all for the sake of making a couple of pounds? Well that's just me when I teach someone about a subject that I'm passionate about. Of course, the other upside to this is people tend to remember it more easily than a random droning of general boringness.

What you'll actually find if you ever met me and had a conversation with me is that I'm the nicest person you could meet. I always hold the door open for other people, help the olds cross the road if they need it, I'm kind, polite, don't lose my temper, shout or abuse others, and I'll always help a friend or family when they need it, no matter what.

You know, in fact, I don't know anyone who's successful that isn't like that in a situation that does not revolve around teaching or business. OK, actually, yeah, thinking about it, I do know one, but 99% of these people are the nicest, kindest, politest people I've ever met. So, there you have it. Just because you see ruthless business owners on TV who may come across negatively in a business situation, you don't have to change yourself personally. It's almost like an on/off switch that you'll develop naturally over time. I just want to put your mind at rest now and point out that it shouldn't affect your personal life.

There is a catch, of course

The catch is that it'll be up to you to prove to the people around you that you haven't changed when you do become a success. All they have to go on is what happens in the media, which isn't exactly a true representation of how things work. Not to worry, this is easy, and I'll explain later on. Now though...

Your Work Hours Matter
And how it effects those around you

Yep, scary thought that when you're striving for success, you have your heart and mind so set on achieving something, even when it's something for those closest to you, it's easy to get lost in it all of it, and forget about them. Look, I'll be honest with you, I made this mistake before. I see those around me making the same mistakes.

Remember I spoke previously about when you've been through something, and you can see someone else take the same path? You can almost predict the future. You can see what's going to happen before it does. That's how it feels when I see someone take this route. I'm here to make sure I'm not walking down the street one day and seeing you doing the same.

So, first up, look at your work hours. It varies massively. If it doesn't yet, when you get going, it sure will. One day might just be an hour or two, and the next day you might run into a problem while launching your product or service, and find that you're awake into the small hours of the morning. My longest stint was a good number of days non-stop (almost four). Don't do that, whatever you do. It's a very weird experience, and not all that healthy.

Anyway, we talked about this earlier so I won't elaborate, but if there's one thing I can advise you to do, it's to warn your friends and family. Just because this is really important to you, and you work on it non-stop, every spare moment, it doesn't mean that anyone else around you has any idea how important it is to you, or what it involves. In fact, I can guarantee they have no idea unless they've been through it themselves.

I did promise not to lecture you about non-business stuff when the book started, but this is one exception that I can't leave out. Even if I left you to experience this on your own, you could lose a lot along the way. That's why I'm telling you about it now.

The very first and most important lesson I ever learned about business, was how to integrate it into my personal life.

Paul Wakefield

Bite Your Tongue But Be Yourself

It only lasts a few minutes

It's amazing, you know, when success hits you, even the smallest way, how those around you change towards you, but if you're careful, it'll only last a few minutes. I started noticing this when I made my first success. Let's see, thinking back, when I first saw those sales coming in at a rapid pace, I was so ecstatic. The moment the cash landed in my account, I had to upgrade my gear. It was so dated by this point.

So, I went out and bought myself a new laptop, a new phone, I grabbed two screens, a printer, and an MP3 player.

Bear in mind I needed the laptop so I could travel, visit family and work at the same time. I needed a new computer because my old one was so dated, hardware wise, it barely ran any of the new software I needed.

The screens were necessary because the contract on my previous ones were so bad, it was hard to work on my graphics projects. The phone, well that's obvious from the above, but that was for work too. Finally, the printer was for my DVD covers for physical products and future projects. The only thing I actually bought for my own enjoyment was the MP3 player.

Anyway, finally my work was done for a couple of weeks, so I invited my best buddy over. Now seeing as we mess about in my office with the computer a little, check out movie trailers and the like on the internet, it was pretty hard to hide. Anyway, he walks in, and the first words that came out his mouth were what I had hoped wouldn't happen. 'You rich *******!' he said. Thankfully, it wore off after about 10 minutes.

Exactly the same happened with my other friends too. The odd joke, and it was over with. No treating anyone differently, no asking for money or trying to take advantage. Nothing. Just a single joke, and that was it. That is, as long as you don't make the fatal mistake of trying to preach to them about what they could do with their lives.

Don't mention money, don't mention how much you earn or how much they earn. Don't try to get them into what you do unless they ask to be involved and are serious long-term, don't mention jobs or promotions unless they begin the conversation. A small price to pay for the massive rewards of owning your own business and having the freedom and lifestyle that you've always dreamed of. Aside from those small anomalies that barely last, I'll be honest with you, nothing much changes.

Friends stay friends, family stay family, and your personality does what you want it to, aided by your diary to keep track of which way you're headed.

Oh, one other thing. When you hit success, some of those around you will suddenly get the urge to try and influence your decisions. I don't know why it happens, but with certain people at certain times, because you're living the perfect life and have a great lifestyle as a result of your hard work, they set their hearts on telling you what you should be doing.

Granted these people are in the minority (at least they are in my circle of friends) but you can always spot it coming before it happens, because they're like that before you hit success, but just to not such an extent. I have no explanation for it, but at least on talking to those that have come along with me on this strange journey to owning their own business, I know for sure I'm not alone.

None of us can explain it. All I'll ask you to remember is the one thing that we spoke about in earlier section, and that's not listening to people who haven't been through the same as you have, especially those that don't even have the slightest connection or a blip of similarity in their life to your projects. All these people are doing is giving you an opinion, even though they'll try and persuade you otherwise.

Usually it's to sell you something, and other times it's for the unknown reason that my friends and I have gone from useless and broke to successful business are yet to be able to explain.

Only listen to those who know what they are talking about, because just as those with opinions can persuade you to see their unfounded guess-like points of view and steer you away from becoming a success, the very same thing can happen when you begin to see success. It's as hard to keep as it is to gain in the first place, just less demanding physically and mentally because you've already learned so much to get you there.

I can give you a million examples of when this happens, but I think just one or two will do. Let's see. Well, the most recent one was when I told some of my online marketing contacts that I was heading in to learn how to invest and make money in property. Just so I have something to do during the summer months and dry periods when not much is going on in my business. I also tend to like working from 4pm onwards, because I get the most done at that time of the day, so I needed something less workload heavy to do during the day.

Anyway, when I first let the news out, I was getting all sorts of responses, varying from congratulations, to words of warning, people telling me about their previous experiences etc. I'm all for that, it's the only way to learn. None of these people had ever been taught by the best in the world before though (which is how I see my mentor. He just the best teacher ever), so I took it all with a pinch of salt.

Next up, I had several people telling me that I shouldn't do it. Telling me how I'll lose all my money like everyone else does, and I'm stupid to get involved and should just stick to one thing that I'm good at. This is that totally random scaremongering that I'm talking about. What if I'd listened to those people when they told me that about online marketing? I wouldn't be here today. I'd still be selling cars and making someone else rich.

So, I took that step, just like you have. What if you'd listened to those telling you that you're stupid for trying? Again, it's that whole thing about the moment you begin to strive for success, break out of the norm and try something new, then certain people suddenly know everything.

They know your future, they know what's going to happen to you, and how well you're going to do, and they try and make you quit it, leave it behind or forget it.

As I said before, if they'd actually been through online marketing, I might well listen to them, but they hadn't, so I didn't, and I made it. That's example one and two in together, because now I'm moving into property investment, those in online marketing are telling me the same. Trying to put me off for some strange reason, again with totally unfounded reasoning, opinions with no experience backing them.

Anyway, they were wrong. Turns out that in my experience, the odds of winning in the property industry is far higher than online marketing. As my mentor says, the property industry is about 20% of the people who know what they're doing getting rich, and taking money from the 80% who don't know what they're doing, who are losing money. I'm pretty sure the odds for online marketing are far longer than one in five. Of course, I can't confirm that, and it is perfectly reasonable to go for success in this field too.

That's enough of the examples, I think. What I hope you can see and learn to recognise, is that no matter what new ground you decide to break, someone, somewhere, who hasn't got a clue will try to stop you. There's always one (sometimes more). It could be family, it could be a friend, it could be some random whiner on the internet that has no clue, it could be a work colleague, it could be one of your contacts, or it could be a random stranger walking down the street. There's always one.

Never listen unless they are an authority. Irrelevant opinions can't influence what you do unless you let them. It'll be your job to figure out if they're unfounded or are a cause for concern.

That's it. That's all of it for this section. We're getting close to the end now. All that's left here is a task, and you're on your way, ready to use everything that you've read, and experience the stories I've talked to you about here for yourself. That was the last knowledge base section aside from the upcoming summary (which is massively important, you should read that too. Far easier to remember everything and pick out highlights).

So, the last task. Let's do it!

"Most people who
ask for advice from
others have already
resolved to act
as it pleases them."

Khalil Gibran

Paul Wakefield

The Last Task
Preparing For Success

I hope you've got that diary by now, because this is where you'll really need it. Now, this task is a little hard, to say the least. Compared to the others anyway; they were the easy ones. See, I track and test everything if you haven't noticed already. I write down my everyday conversations, what I've learned, what I did well, what I did badly, what my experiment was, and what it's going to be tomorrow, and any other ideas for future entries, and how other people react to my changes. I have the most fun with that one.

Anyway, you can do all of this too, if you like. It only takes one A4 page of text every day before you head to bed. That's something else to put in your shiny new diary. The amount that it helps is absolutely immense. Every little thing you'll see coming before it happens, so much so it's almost like you can shape the future predictably and very easily, just by watching yourself and others on a daily basis, and noting down any patterns that may occur.

In my final attempt to get those of you that haven't got a journal up and running yet, and for those of you that don't necessarily have the time to spend before you head to bed writing a full A4 page of text, I can safely say, you don't need to write everything down, just the important bits. Some suggestions for you include a personal diary, if you want to improve that part of your life, or a business diary, if you want to improve that part. You can do a trading diary if you're trading on the stock market, or doing anything else that you believe to be important. All you have to do is note down the important bits.

Now this is that good bit that I wanted to get to. This whole diary thing can be used in a massive number of ways. One of those ways is to squash any fears about the future. You've heard the saying that those that aren't successful aren't ready to be successful, I'm sure (or something along those lines), but as far as that goes, there's not some super cosmic energy holding them back or anything like that. It's their fears and their excuses.

What did we establish was the number one fear of those wanting to be successful? Of course, how they'll change as a person when they get there. You can get rid of that right now if you're worried about it. First things first, note down who you look up to and what you respect and admire about them. Secondly, when you're done, note down your top five interpersonal personality traits that you're proud of, and then five things you'd like to change. All it is, is a record for yourself. You can come back later and see how much you've changed. And, if you have changed and you don't like it, what you have in front of you is a blueprint for being how you used to be. Easy.

I'm sure you're going to be surprised just how similar to your old self you are, and just how subtle the changes need to be to take you all the way through to absolute success.

Of course, if you started your diary already, you won't have this fear, because you're making little corrections along the way from your daily records.

So, there we go. Last try.

Diary!

Paul Wakefield

"The only source of knowledge is experience."

Albert Einstein

CHAPTER SEVEN
We've Come to the End of the Line

This is Where I Leave You

Wow, what a ride. I have to say, I totally enjoyed writing every single word of this. I hope it showed too, and you found it interesting and got something out of it. Don't worry though, just because I'm leaving you here, it doesn't mean it's the end of the road. The changes that we've talked about aren't just something you can implement today and see results from. The more you use them, the better the results will be.

Have a think about what you just learned over the past six chapters too, and just how important they are and how much information they contain.

Look at it this way, everything here is as a result of my work and experiments over many years. None of it has come from memory at all. Memories get distorted and just aren't accurate enough, which is why I took everything from what I wrote down and tested.

I hope no one dismisses anything because I was young when I started. Remember, I didn't actually start using any of this until I was out of school. It was all just a bit of fun, one big experiment up until then. I had no idea that it would mean the difference between being totally lost as to how to get out of a bad situation (probably taking years to figure it out) and finally end up being the basis for my success.

My aim for this book was to create something interesting to read, and fun, challenging and rewarding to take part in. That's where the tasks came in. I also put it together in such a way that anyone who decided to implement these methods into their businesses, or any other aspect of their life, results would be immediate, and keep rewarding the user the more they used them.

For those of you who followed along with me, I hope you're seeing some changes in your life and your business already.

Something else I want to say before we get to the summary, is that everyone is different. During my experiments, I tested the methods I talked to you about here tens, even hundreds, of times with many different people over many years.

The results have always stayed the same and they have worked for me. I'm confident in all of them, however, and even though the majority (if not all of them) will work for the majority of people, there may be one or two that don't work as well as they do or have done in the past for me.

This is why I've been going on and on at you all throughout these pages to start your own diary. I mean, there's only one way to find out if they work – to put them into action, and to test them out. A journal is probably the least statistical, least boring way to do this. It's also really easy to refer back to at a later date if you lose something you've had before. That way, you know what you did to get it in the first place, and can repeat the process and are most likely see the same results.

This has been the whole idea, of course. Do start that journal though. It really is invaluable, and I sure wouldn't go on about it so much if it wasn't so much of road map to success for me. It doesn't take years either. Within a week, you'll already have made several observations about particular situations yourself and know what to do to replicate previous experiences, all from doing something as simple as jotting down your thoughts.

Unlike memories, of course, it never gets distorted either. An accurate representation of past events and lessons learned in your hand. There is nothing in the world that is more powerful for changing your future. It's done more for me than I could ever express to you in a million pages of text.

Oh, one last thing. I hope I didn't scare anyone off in the early sections with the self-help bashing. It was really so people remember what I said the next time they come across one of these books. Whether they believe it or not, at least they'll have a think about it.

Especially that point about confidence destroyers, and those with too much belief in the 'sit back and do nothing' methods losing the confidence and power to pull themselves out of inevitable tough situations. Anyway, I hope I didn't offend anyone. Apologies if I did. That doesn't mean I didn't mean every single word of it.

Paul Wakefield

To sum up, this whole book has been about one single point. Handing power back to you. Your future, so you control what you're going to achieve. The decisions you make, every single little thing you do daily, from maintenance, pro-activity, reactivity, every e-mail, every word on a sales letter, every product idea and development:

You're in control of your success.

Nobody else.

Feels good, doesn't it?

"Learn from the past,
set vivid, detailed goals
for the future,
and live in the only moment
of time over which you have
any control:
now."

Denis Waitley

The Summary
Making things easy to commit to memory

- The whole success of this book depends on understanding, knowledge, improvement, efficiency, and action on your part, not praying, mantras, or mystical powers. Action is the key.

- Using this book is easy. The knowledge is split up into six chapters. Take the information in as you feel comfortable doing so. Don't rush it, especially not when applying each aspect that could well take days, weeks or even months to implement fully ('fully' being when it becomes a habit, and you no longer have to force yourself to do it).

- The first step to success is changing the way you think about it. It's not something you have to do. If you think like that, you'll do everything you can to avoid it. Instead, you have to want to do it.

- It's easy to change your thoughts about working on your business and breaking new ground. When you give yourself the freedom not to do it, you're in control, and you can pick what you want to do and how often, you'll find yourself starting to actually want to do jobs you avoided previously, or have found hard in the past. Everything is your choice and will continue to be throughout this whole book.

- This book is different for five reasons. One, I'm not telling you how to run your life or forcing info on you. Second, I've tested this information for many years and over 1,000 experiments in the business field. Third, I am a normal person who began with one set of clothes, paper, and a pen.

That's all. I know how to go from nothing to something. Four, you don't have to wait for it. Each section has a task you can act on and begin to see immediate results. Finally, five, practical application. I'll show you when, where and how I figured all of this out, where I use it in my business, and where you can use it.

- Self-help got It wrong. Lesson number one, any concept where you can sit back and let everything come to you will not work long-term for several reasons. Don't fall for it. They're just telling you what you want to hear and we all know it. You risk damaging your confidence by thanking cosmic forces for your success. It was you who did the hard work and achieved. Understand this now, and when the next downer hits, you will have the belief in yourself you need to get up, that those that fall for self-help severely lack.

- It takes development and understanding to learn what it takes to get rich and then keep it. You being willing to search for information about the subject puts you firmly on the right track. A very good head start.

- Believing in yourself is the key to success. It's proved itself again and again throughout my diaries. Confidence. This is the one thing that the 'sit back and wait for it to come to you' books do well.

- Gaining confidence is easy. All you have to do is recognise it when you do something good. Give yourself a pat on the back, say, 'Well done, all that hard work paid off, congratulations on your achievement'. Pat yourself on the back for every little thing that you do well, no matter how small it may seem, you are achieving, and making progress. This is what's important.

- You started already and should be proud. Look at those around you. How many of them opted to work for someone else? How many don't like

No Excuses, No Limits

their financial situation and their lifestyle? How many are doing something about it? By picking up this book, you've taken an extraordinary step already.

- Only do this when you do something good though. Congratulating yourself on a job not well done defeats the object of this exercise. Numbing yourself with mindless self-complimenting will stop you from recognising mistakes. Without that, you can't improve and learn from previous experiences.

- When attempting to learn a new skill, attach yourself to someone who has been in a similar situation and reached a point that you would really like to reach also. The comments of your friends, family and colleagues are just opinions, unless they've made it and can teach you how to get there. People like to think they know it all nowadays, even though they have no quantifiable, recorded and proven results. They'll lead you off in the wrong direction if you start listening to them. Learn to define between fact, from someone who's been there, and opinion, from those who whether they have your best interests at heart, probably don't know what they're talking about.

- Set goals for the future, both long-, medium- and short-term. You can mix in business with personal, if you like. It's entirely up to you. Where will you be in a week? In a month? Six months? A year? Five years?

- Create an image book to help visualise goals. Write down the date you came up with the goal, a little descriptive passage about the goal itself, and the best picture or photo you can find. It's much easier to accept when a picture is attached to it.

- Don't be taken in. Remember that only those who are where you want to be and have come from where you're coming from (situation wise) know what it'll take for you to be a success. No one's opinions should sway you.

• The most powerful forms of marketing include the dredges of human society's moods and feelings. Greed, jealousy, hate, frustration, anxiety, fear. Some choose the other route of love, happiness, bliss, hope, joy, getting the things you want with the least effort. You're in business and will be hit by these methods. Look closely at whether their methods are viable and if they'll work. Don't let them make you kid yourself into thinking something is easier than it is. As the old saying goes, 'If it looks too good to be true, it probably is'. It could set you back years, and in the worst cases, destroy your confidence.

• Stay focused. Move furniture around to give your house or apartment that shiny new feeling, reminding yourself how good change feels. Remove distractions, TVs, and anything that will take your attention away. Couple this with regular breaks (instead of massive boring work stints lasting hours) and you'll be able to concentrate on your work for much longer without a hundred other things vying for your attention.

• Making progress vs maintenance. If you're working hard and not getting much done, check your activities. Are you maintaining, tidying, cleaning and fixing what was messed up that day? Or are you being proactive and moving forward? Without pro-activity, there is no progress. Without progress, there's no reaching your goals. A daily journal entry really helps keep track of this.

Summary One

- Always have a vision of your future lifestyle, but never have a vision of the process that will take you there. Just because you can see a perfect business working and work towards it, doesn't mean that it'll be a viable business in the end. Your plans will most likely be totally unrecognisable by the time you reach the end. Dream about the end result, it will keep you going. Take the process as it comes and adapt it daily. This will keep you out of the maintenance pit, where you find yourself in the same chair, doing the same jobs a year later.

- There are three methods for success. Number one is the outright stubbornness. Don't listen to anyone; no matter what they say, go for it anyway. The plus side is you smash through barriers and make progress. The potential to achieve something beyond all expectations is there and readily happens. The downside is you may expend massive amounts of energy and draw a blank, and not know why. Devastating seeing as you won't know to not make the same mistake again.

- Number two, listen to others and act on their thoughts and comments. The plus side is you get to see things from another perspective, and avoid any problems that you might not have foreseen. The downside is there's so many opinions out there, barely any of it is fact. You end up guided away in the wrong direction by people who think they know what they're talking about, but actually have never experienced anything that comes close to your situation, nothing on the way to reaching your goals, and have never and probably will never reach their own.

- Number three. The ideal situation. A bit of both. You use the stubbornness method to tear through the rubbish that won't help you. You drive in a straight line, and you drive hard, destroying all obstacles in your way. You no longer take any thoughts or opinions into account from anyone - friends, family, or colleagues - that doesn't have the facts and have trodden the path that you're trading, because let's face it, they're just guessing. How can they know what you need to progress when they're further behind you on the road to success? Impossible.

- Begin a journal as soon as you can. It'll allow you to keep an eye on your progress, and run your own experiments. Who knows where it'll take you in the future. Maybe you'll be writing a book like this of your own?

Summary Two

- Failure is not taboo. It's not something to be afraid of. When you fail, you learn something to be applied on the next attempt, meaning you're far more likely to succeed. You can't lose unless you stop taking action.

- Don't see failure as unacceptable. No one has ever not failed. Accept it, learn from it, and simply move on. You can't change the past. We all know that. Very few people act on that knowledge and live in the past. Brush it off, say, 'Oh well,' not, 'Oh no!'

- Looking at the past is imperative. Never listen to someone who tells you to ignore it, because it's self-defeating. You'll find yourself in limbo, making the same mistakes over and over again, and making very little progress. Failing and lack of success is the most vital learning tool we have, and yet, there are those out there telling you to ignore it.

- Another note about not being taken in. If you think hard enough about it, it will happen. Rubbish. Don't be afraid to be negative sometimes. It's totally unnatural to be happy and positive all the time. It's blind, it's short-sighted, and all that happy positive thinking is pulling you away from recognising the things you should be changing to fix your situation.

- When looking at your past and your mistakes with a view to learn, don't get stuck and dwell on it. Learning from your mistakes is powerful, but it's a dangerous game. Do you quit business because your last start-up failed? No. If you fail to achieve a goal, you don't drop that goal altogether and deem that you can't do it. Instead, you change the process and the methods in which you're using. The goals stay the same.

- Many of the successful I meet fail more than they succeed, yet they still get rich. Think of the stock market trader who loses on more trades than he wins on. Think of the search engine marketer who loses on 90% of the keywords he attempts. Think of myself, as the consultant who has failed with a number of big contracts. How do they all get rich by failing more than succeeding? Cutting their losses. If it sucks, don't try and maintain it and push it along for years. Ditch it and start again. Replace it with something that works quickly. This is how the successful get rich, even when they lose more times than they win. They ditch the money losers very quickly, and let the ones that make the money roll on and keep making money.

Summary Three

- Learning is the underlying basis of success. If you aren't learning, you can't move forwards towards your goals, because you'll always make the same mistakes. This is the way most business owners go. This is not the way you will be going after reading this.

- Learning to learn in the real world is very different to what we all experienced in our school days. The majority of the time, our teachers were well trained and had an outline of what they wanted to teach us, culminating in an exam that tests what we remember from our lessons. In the real world, however, everyone likes to be the teacher and know everything, whether it's to impress you, to get you on their lists, or to take money out of your pocket. Sadly, most of these teachers express opinion, not fact, and they'll probably not be caught for years, as it won't become obvious until then whether they were taking you for a ride, or teaching you something valuable.

- I tested these methods wherever I could. In online marketing, in offline marketing, in my personal life, sports and hobbies. Everything fell into place, and I was becoming successful at things in mere months that those hadn't managed to do after many years of attempts. Take these into account, even if you've heard the following before. If you're not making rapid progress, you're not making full use of this knowledge.

- Attach yourself to someone who is an authority on your chosen subject. Don't waste time on opinions. Look for someone who has come from a similar background as yourself, and has reached a goal you want to reach. Pick more than one if you want, but make sure they all have similar backgrounds and plans for the future.

- If you're striving for success with a small budget and little time, find someone who was in the same situation as you to learn how to get it all. If you're a success already, or were born in to wealth, find someone in the same situation as you to learn how to keep it all. These two require very different approaches. Mix and match doesn't work all that well because of this.

- Spend your money on their products once you've established who has valuable information. Buy everything they sell, learn from it, put it into action, and if you've chosen wisely, you should see immediate results. It's far less painful and risky to buy from someone you've researched and look up to as a role model for success, than it is to buy from a stranger and hope they know what they're talking about.

- Watch other marketers and business owners for changing trends, but don't get wrapped up in them. Stick to your chosen subjects until you've learned everything you can from them and feel you have matched or surpassed them. You will see some very powerful marketing come your way. Try to resist being side-tracked. Focus

Summary Four

- Opportunity is everywhere. The key to taking advantage of it is learning to spot it, which most people cannot do. The next person you speak to could literally change your life. Situations can change in mere minutes, if not seconds. Don't feel trapped. Change is never far off if you know where to look.

- Keep your path fluid. Plan your final destination (your goal) but keep that journey plan adaptable. New shortcuts can pop up in front of your eyes every day. Plan well, but don't be afraid to deviate and test.

- Six degrees of separation states that each person in the world (including you) is connected to everyone else by just six other people. A friend of a friend of a friend. Imagine how much power you wield if this is true. I personally think something similar is true, but I have a feeling it's more like ten than six. Either way, when you have the whole world at your fingertips, it doesn't really matter if it's one or 100 steps, it's still out there, yours for the taking.

- There are two methods for making new contacts. One thing you have to remember when doing this is what most networking guys and gals forget. It's that it has to go both ways. You can't expect to be introduced to people and not do the same for others. Often it's not a direct exchange, contact for contact, but it keeps things moving quickly if you use method one extensively.

- Method one, force the situation. If you see someone with a strength and another with a weakness with a common goal, play matchmaker and hook them up. You'd be amazed at what you get in return in regards to new contacts, even if others don't know about forcing the situation and only using method number two.

- Method two, let it all happen. Tell people about yourself, preferably business if you want to get more business contacts. Word of mouth as a marketing tool is massively powerful, and word will spread. You will make more contacts even if the people you tell know nothing about these methods, simply because of the, 'Oh! I know someone who's into business too!' effect. Something that happens regularly in conversations that we take for granted. Next time you hear someone say something like that, you've just witnessed this in action.

- Don't use people. They are not just going to make you rich. They will make the journey easier, but you have to start walking down that road first, or you won't be able to make use of these opportunities.

Summary Five

- You can improve your lifestyle right away. All it takes is an hour or two of shopping. You'll want to do this as soon as you possibly can too. We can't have you getting rich and being too sick to enjoy it long-term.

- Mental and physical strains of learning a new skill with a view to running a business is very different from school. In school, you had set things to remember. You were told them, you wrote them down, drew diagrams, and then you were tested on what you remember. Here, we're assimilating new habits, new timetables, and sometimes even new personality traits. We're judged on actions, not what we remember about a subject. This is why it's important to stay in top condition and look after yourself. You'll feel mighty drained after just a few months if you neglect this.

- One step at a time. Don't try and change your business, your diet, quit smoking, lose weight, be successful at search social media marketing, get good at JV marketing, learn how about property investment, run an offline business and juggle family life at the same time. Learning is tough here. Stick to one at a time and you'll succeed far faster than if you were trying to climb the ladder missing out every rung in between the bottom and the top.

- Order your tasks and the changes you want to make sensibly. The one you're carrying out should always help the next in line. An example: gain the confidence to be successful in business, get successful in business and earn enough to double success and speed up the process by investing, then quit smoking when there's less worries, then with the extra money and free time, added comfort and lifestyle additions, treat yourself to a change in diet to 100% fresh, organic and free-range food.

- Look after your body. Flat screen monitor for your eyes, the ultimate comfortable office chair for your stints in front of your computer, light, non splinted wrist supports to promote blood flow after typing, lift your wrists off the keyboard when typing and avoid stretching, and sleep when you feel like it. All things you could do right now.

- Remove instances of work from your sleep and recreation areas. You don't want to begin to associate these areas with work. It's hard enough to get business out of our minds as it is without having a computer staring you in the face when you're trying to sleep, generating all sorts of ideas and thoughts that will keep you from relaxing. A good excuse to turn that spare room into a study. If you can't go that far, cover the computer up at least.

Summary Six

- Change scares people. It makes them nervous. If you feel nervous about what's going on, that's a good sign. That means you've done something different from what you're used to. If your situation isn't all that favourable, you know this change will most likely be good. Stick with it. Don't let the jittery feelings stop you from making progress.

- You can never know it all, even when you're at the top of your game. Be careful when talking to people about your knowledge. Only give correct information, and information they ask for.

- Don't preach. Just because you're brave enough to dive head on into owning your own business, it doesn't mean anyone else will dare, or even want to give it a shot. If they ask you for business advice, so be it, feel free to help them. Don't force change on those who aren't ready.

- Success doesn't have to change you as a person. Keep an eye on your diary entries and watch the situation. If you see something you don't like, you can look back to previous entries and get an immediate blueprint showing you the way back.

- The media isn't all there is. These grumpy business owners you see on TV that everyone loves to hate and throw insults at doesn't have to be you. It probably isn't even what they're like as a person outside of business situations. You can get rich and still be a kind, happy and friendly person.

- People may think you're going to change. It's a common myth that the business person is a selfish person who hates everything but their precious money. It's up to you to prove them wrong, because all they've had experience with here is in the media. Not exactly an accurate representation of a personality, especially not when you only see them in front of a camera in business situations.

- Your work hours can be long, and they can change frequently when you own your own business, or even when you're striving for success in a non-business sense. Remember to warn those around you and explain what's happening, or you might find yourself returning to reality years later, massively rich, but no one to enjoy it with. Heed this warning if you heed no other in this book.

- Comments from friends and family will come from all around about your newfound success. If you're in business, this could well be about the money. Thing is, while it might seem like they're complimenting you from their point of view, it won't be something you want to bring up in conversation very often. Just brush it off, and move on. After a couple of comments, and a few minutes, everything will be back to normal. Only those who tried to take advantage of you before you were a success will try to do so when you are a success.

- Don't be too suspicious of your friends' comments. After all, they don't know how to act around someone who is a complete and utter success. It'll take them some time to learn, so go easy.

Last Words
Well, that's it.

No more writing for me to do on this subject =(I did enjoy it immensely though. If there's one final piece of advice I can give you, it's that not every reader will like what they've heard, but there is very likely to be at least one method in here that you do like. Take that as a starting point. It's all up to you now. You know that success is out there waiting for you; opportunity is everywhere. You know how to find it, how to act on it, and how to react to the people around you when you get it.

It's all yours. Stop making EXCUSES and go get it.

I wish you all the best on your journey.

P.S. One word: Journal.

Paul Wakefield

OK, so I didn't want to leave you like I did, so decided to include these extra pages for you with a combination of the previous pictures.

So, why did I include those pictures of me out in India, you might be asking.

Well, for two reason really.

Reason one is because I wanted to share my love and passion of India. As some of you may already know, in 2012 thanks to implementing everything that I've shared with you in this book, I was able to spend three months travelling around India and these are just a very small choice of pictures that I wanted to share with you.

Reason two, thanks to what I achieved, I'm now in a position that allows me to donate 5% of my profit to a charity out in India. Now I'm not just meaning profit from this book, I mean profit from my business.

I just want to say a massive thank you for buying this book as your donation with make a BIG impact on the charity that I support.

The Importance of Goals in Our Life

Goals lead us to a fruitful life. Without them, we are like just plain logs in the forest standing uselessly. With goals, we become trees that bear fruits. We become meaningful for others and in ourselves.

These goals have to be clearly stated and detailed for us for follow. Otherwise, goals that are vague lead us nowhere.

Once we have the clear goals, we have to find people we respect to serve as a compass who would tell us if we are on our right track in crafting our goals and later on whether we are achieving the goals we have earlier set.

One of the details in coming with a defined goal is the time frame at each step one has to make in order to reach the highest goal. These steps have to be measurable in order for us to know if we are moving along the path.

Keep goals simple and reasonable. A too bold and aggressive goal that is impossible to achieve would only nurture discontentment. We would abandon these goals later on. Likewise, we should also not come up with goals that are too easy to achieve because the challenge would not be there that would push us to achieve and feel fulfilled once we achieved the goals.

The steps sound like a business development plan, but this time it is applied to your life. Start by writing down important things you would like to attain in your life.

Once you have written these things, set out a plan to achieve the goals and commit to the plan. Remember to set milestones on your schedules. Get other people involved to witness your journey and success in achieving your plan. These people will be there to see that you accomplish your plan in coaching and supporting you, even when you feel discouraged.

Get them involved in making you achieve your plan. For you to achieve your goal, you need all the resources you need to work together in getting you there.

Setting goals can be an easy task for many people. However, achieving the goals set is not always so easy. For example, anyone can say, 'I am going to lose 10 pounds this month.' Saying it is easy; doing it is difficult. Meeting your goals takes dedication, drive, and motivation. Below are three proven strategies for successful goal setting.

1. Keep Your Goals Realistic

One of the most important elements of setting goals is to keep them realistic. You would not want to set a goal to complete an upcoming marathon, if you're not an experienced runner. Those kinds of goals are more like wishes than goals, because they are nearly impossible to achieve. A more realistic goal could be to enter a half marathon and focus on finishing the race, or tackle a smaller version. The danger of setting unrealistic goals is that you're not likely to achieve them. This can affect your motivation to try something new in the future.

2. Write Goals Down

When you set personal goals for yourself, you are more likely to achieve them if you have written them down. There are several reasons why writing down your goals is an effective tool, and they are:

- Provides clarity
- Strengthens motivation
- Keeps you accountable
- Builds self-esteem

When people write down their goals, they have a much greater degree of success in achieving them. It's also an excellent visual reminder to keep you focused, when goals are posted in places you'll see every day.

3. Remain Positive

When you are working toward your goals, you're likely to encounter a few challenges along the way. This is perfectly normal. In order to move through your challenges more quickly, stay focused on the positive effect achieving the goal will have on your life and consider the following:

- Rewarding yourself for reaching milestones
- Visualising your success
- Reading your goal list daily

Achieving your personal goals can heighten your self-esteem and improve your overall quality of life. If you set realistic goals, write them down, and remain positive; you are much more likely to achieve the goals you set.

Paul Wakefield

Should You Dream Big, Or Be More Realistic?

We had vivid imaginations as children. As an adult, have you lost some of that childlike ability to imagine the future?

Is the ability to dream big a valuable goal setting/achieving skill or an unrealistic time waster?

When it comes to setting and achieving goals, I often see coaching clients divided into two groups - the dreamers and the realists. The dreamers are reaching for the stars and the realists are going for the sure thing. Which is the best approach for setting and achieving goals? In my opinion, it is a combination of both. Here's what I believe:

The Dreamer: It is an asset to be able to focus on the future. To vividly see what you want and to picture how you're going to achieve it. Sometimes though, the dreamers don't realise their limitations. On the positive side, the dreamers are excellent at creating goal achieving affirmations and visualizations.

The Realist: They know their strength and weaknesses. They have a firm grasp on what works and what doesn't work. Often though, they will stop themselves from coming out of their preconceived comfort zone. The realist is excellent at mapping out step-by-step and day-by-day plans for achieving their goals.

The Realistic Dreamer: They have a down-to-earth ability to dream big and bold. The realistic dreamer knows how to set goals that stretch beyond their current comfort zone and yet, they don't find themselves getting discouraged with frustrating and unworkable expectations.

Here are a few examples:

The Dreamer: A five foot five adult person whose goal is to stretch and become a six feet seven professional basketball player is unrealistic. A more realistic goal may be to play basketball for fun and also spend time coaching others who love the game.

The Realist: The middle-aged mother who wants to go back to school but is sure that she has lost her edge. She's been out of school for many years and refuses to enrol in college classes. A more realistic approach would be to take one class at the local community college or an adult education course to help her feel more comfortable learning and growing within a structured environment.

The Realistic Dreamer: The woman in business who decides to expand her business into a foreign country, although she has never been outside of the United Kingdom. She develops a business plan and then seeks out a mentor or coach who is knowledgeable in foreign commerce. This entrepreneur reads, learns and begins growing toward her dream, one positive step at a time. A realistic dreamer does not allow uncertainty or insecurity to stop them from setting goals. However, they do realise that coming out of a comfort zone means seeking out advice, help and support.

Becoming a realistic dreamer is about knowing what you want to achieve, why you want to achieve it and being able to map out a viable and doable plan of action. Combining the childlike ability to dream with a realistic assessment of what can be done is a powerful and extremely valuable goal achieving skill.

Which are you; the dreamer, the realist, or the realistic dream?

Paul Wakefield

How to Simply Simplify your Life

It's kind of funny how people get when they decide that they need to simplify their life. Instead of figuring out an easy and relaxed way to do this, they freak out over it. They make all sorts of massive lists, all sorts of pie charts and Venn diagrams. They read 30 books on the subject, and eventually end up complicating their life tenfold in their attempt to simplify it. Think about it this way; doesn't it make sense that a system that will effectively help you simplify your life will be, well, simple?

The first easy step towards effectively simplifying your life is sitting down and making the smallest list possible about what you find to be most important in your life. Don't do this on your computer. A txt or Word document is potentially infinite in size, and this will make it possible to make a massive list, or to use a complicated process to create your list. Instead, just take a regular piece of paper (either ruled or computer sheets) and fold it up a couple of times. Ideally, you want to only give yourself space to write five things down. Figure out what the top five commitments are, the five most important factors in your life are. Think about what you value, think about what makes you most happy to spend your time on, think about what helps you grow and move forward in your life. Figuring out your priorities is the most important thing to do.

Once you know what your priorities are, subtract one from the list. Go through, figure out what's least important to you, and then remove it from the list. Chances are there's at least one item on your list that you put down there because you feel obligated to rank it as a top priority, even if it brings you neither joy nor progress in your life. Don't kid yourself, and cut the emotional hold it has on you now by removing it from your list. You will not have a mostly accurate list of what's most important in your life. Focus on these things to the exclusion of everything else. Do what you need to so that you can pay your bills and what not, but do the minimum to fulfil your obligations and the maximum to pursue your priorities.

Now that you've made an emotional and intellectual commitment to that which really matters to you in your life, you need to make it a physical reality. Go through your life and remove those things that don't contribute to your priorities and that aren't needs, like earning enough money to fund your life. Clean out your desk, clean out your drawers, clean out your computer desktop, your inboxes and your to-do lists. Remove all those things that are simply weighing you down and doing nothing for what really is important to you. Just purge those things in your life that will continuously be associated with unimportant aspects of your life. For those items and folders that are related to your financial and other necessary obligations, put them out of sight when you're not using them. For everything else, make sure what you see at all times has a positive association.

Now that you've decided what's important and cleared out space for it in your life, I'm going to make one last suggestion. Look over your list of priorities. If one of them is having a fulfilling social life, then great. You need to be with people to be happy in your life; you can't just be an focused goal machine at all times. If enjoyable human interaction is nowhere on the list, then remove the least important thing remaining on your list and replace it with leaving your house and enjoying your life with people you love.

Paul Wakefield

The Power of Gratitude

Gratitude is the use of the Power of Thought in a way that will put you in Harmony with the Energy of the Universe. The same way that there is a Law of Attraction, there is a Law of Gratitude. You must learn to use this Law in order for the Law of Attraction to work.

The Law of Gratitude works this way. When you give thanks or praise for the things you already have, you make way for more to come to you because you are thankful. The Law of Gratitude is a Natural Law and will always respond in a Like Nature. Remember, Reaction and Action are always equal. The response you receive will be the same as you send out.

What this means is the Universe will give you more of the good things you deserve because you are thankful for all the good things you already have. As you give thanks for what you have, you are saying that you are happy and pleased with what you have attained thus far. You appreciate the better things in life, and want and deserve more. The Energy of the Universe will comply with this, bringing more of the better things into existence.

You want the best in life; the best that life has to offer. Think these thoughts in your mind, and feel the best feelings that you can feel. See yourself with the best; the best of everything and that is what the Law of Attraction and the Law of Gratitude will produce.

Be Grateful for everything good that comes into your life, and more will come into your life as well. Be thankful every time you get a chance throughout your day. Expect the best; expect good things, and you will receive the best and more good things. Showing Gratitude will bring more things into your life to be Grateful for. Where is your future heading? If you really take the time to answer this question, you will find that your future is within you. Within You, is the Power and Energy to change your Destiny?

Everything you see and touch, everything surrounding you, from the air you breathe, the food you eat, to the sun you feel on your skin, is made up of Energy. Think of the Love you feel when you hold a hand. Think of the way you feel when you kiss a child. The deep inner emotions and feelings that drive our consciousness. This is your Life; this is created by your thoughts, your energy.

Imagine what it would be like if you looked out on the vast ocean and didn't see any water. Now think about how you would feel if you never saw a star. What would the world be like if there was no music? What if, tomorrow, all the trees were gone, every blade of grass, and every plant and flower dried up and blew away?

What would the world look like then? How would a future artist ever paint a landscape? Where would we be if there were no animals? What would you eat if there were no fruits and vegetables? How many salads can you make with dirt?

We take for granted this world, this life, and this wonderful place where we live. God planned it all, every last grain of sand. Every plant and every animal, every fish and every seed, and He did it with His Mind, with His Thoughts, with His Intentions. Be Grateful. Start using the Energy. Start right now! Think of the future you want to have. Visualise and picture it in your mind. Start feeling good about it, and know that it is yours. Know that you deserve it. Know that the Universe will create it for you in Abundance.

Paul Wakefield

Secrets to Staying Happy

The reason why many people are living miserable instead of happy lives is because they miss the entire point of why they exist. They focus too much on the less important things (which they think should be prioritised). This article will show you how to fix your eyes on the more important things so that you can have the kind of life you want to live.

Thinking too much about keeping the house perfectly cleaned will just stress you out, so I suggest you take a break from cleaning the house. It's important that your house is free from dust and dirt, but you don't necessarily have to perform a general clean every day. The house will still get cleaned, if not today, so relax.

While you're taking a break from your housekeeping duties, find a way to hang out with your friends and loved ones. Be a child or a teenager again. You used to spend hours talking and laughing with your friends, so why stop now just because you've grown to become an adult? You can be an adult, and still have the heart and mind of a little child.

Never, ever do multiple things at the same time. You're not a Pentium 4 processor, so why try to accomplish 10 tasks in one sitting? Do things one step at a time. I'm not promoting laziness; I'm just saying you would probably be able to get things done if you don't multi-task. Again, I say, relax and enjoy what you're doing.

Having so many accomplishments doesn't make one happy. It may even add up to your insecurities in life. If you really want to learn the secrets of staying happy, talk to someone you know who is contented with his or her life. I know this is a cliché, but being contented with your life is really what's going to make you happy.

Your life doesn't go on forever, my friend. Even if you don't get more things done today, it's OK. What's important is that you enjoy what you have in life; your spouse, your children, your friends and even your career.

Be Happy And Stay Happy All The Time!

Why You're Not Happy

Do you dare to love each moment as if it were your last?

Does your heart fill with tears every time you awaken to live a new day?

Does your heart drop to its knees at every sunset, every song?

No grand activities are required to express your reverence for every moment. In fact, it may be the simple and the mundane - imbued with a sense of awe and wonder - that fills your life with joy.

If good things come to you, and your life is filled with blessings, then savour every moment - and don't overlook the joy of simply being alive.

Nothing is guaranteed. Every relationship, every experience, every success, is an offering from life. But life itself is the greatest offering!

YOU ARE ALIVE!

Taste it, love it, honour it - for it could be taken away in a flash.

Don't lose yourself in plans for the future without first falling in love with this moment - right now.

This moment - life itself - contains within it the deepest fulfilment you could wish for. And all it requires is for you to fall in love with it.

Discover the endless depth in gratitude - gratitude for life itself - and you will always be happy. Happiness will hunt you down and invade you. It will break into every cell and never leave you.

Never stop loving. Love for a reason, for sure. And love without a reason too. And say thank you for everything, even when it seems crazy.

If you're not happy, it's because you forgot that to be alive is the greatest gift. If you're not happy, it's because you forgot to feel eternally grateful for every breath. If you're not happy, it's because you forgot to fall in love with life itself.

You have the power to live a life of undying joy. Start now by saying thank you - with humility and devotion - say thank you for simply being alive. And then see if there's anything you need to simply be happy...

How Peace of Mind can help you Create Prosperity

There are so many things that get in the way of our experiencing prosperity in our lives, but the most important thing we can do is to develop a prosperity consciousness. By the time we get to midlife, we have a tendency to look too much to our past and sometimes it stops us from revealing our good.

Here are some simple thoughts to raise your consciousness about money in midlife and beyond.

1. Focus your energy on the good that is already in your life. When you focus on what you already have, rather than what appears to be missing, your imagination is freed to develop more. Focus is the most important ingredient of any manifestation. You cannot just do affirmations for a few minutes and then spend the rest of the day worrying. Peace brings prosperity, not the other way around.

2. Do whatever it takes to convince yourself that you will make it; no matter where you have been, today is a new day and the past does not equal the future.

3. By now, you may have gathered that there are many ways to earn money. You might want to start by making a list of at least 10 ways that you could earn money now if you had to. Let your imagination soar. Soaring in mind, yields soaring in pounds.

4. Watch the thoughts you may have about having to borrow money now or in the past. Allow money to circulate.

5.   Worry will never produce more. And worry is not only limited to those who have little. Choose to release worry from your life, regardless of the appearances.

OK, some of this sounds like it may go against what you are used to thinking. But it is important to feed your mind with lots of positive and new understandings about prosperity and its true source. If you go now to http://www.paul-wakefield.co.uk you will find several articles and videos that can support the process of change. There's even a course you can take that will take away all fear around money.

How to Become More Positive To Attract A Better Life

We all know that we have to be positive and, more importantly, feel positive to attract the things we want to manifest in life. But how do we change our negative beliefs and our outlook on life that we have believed for so long? We just have to keep learning and putting that knowledge to use for our advantage.

We all know how to effectively manifest stuff we don't want into our life. Being late, getting the wrong order at a restaurant, and not have things turn out the way we wanted it to turn out. We expect these things to happen on a daily basis and then we exclaim, 'I knew that was going to happen!' or 'Why do bad things always happen to me?' but we don't realise that thinking like that is the very thing that is holding us back from manifesting our dreams.

Those common phrases add negativity in our lives and they almost become a staple in our lives - two things that do not help us become more positive about life.

So, how do we become more positive? The solution is to flip these negative sayings around and start exclaiming things like, 'It always works out for me!' or, 'Great things happen to me every day!' and get rid of the negative sayings altogether.

It feels weird to talk positive like that, right? But why should it? Why is it so easy to talk negative and so hard to talk positive?

It stems from our beliefs, which stem from our experiences, which ultimately stem from what we've been taught in life.

We've been taught that life is hard and bad things happen to good people, and because we have manifested those bad things over and over again into our life, we believe that it must be true. It becomes easier and easier for us to attract bad things to us because with each negative experience we believe it's going to happen more and more.

Soon we start to believe that we can't have what we really want. The perfect home, job, spouse, house, and so on and so forth, become far-fetched and hopeless so instead of trying again, we spend our lives saying more of those common negative sayings like, 'You can't always get what you want!' We have to learn to wake up and realise that all of that is complete crap.

All we have to do is change the way we talk and think and talk about life and its rules and make those new thought into our beliefs. That's it.

Those beliefs will then change the way your life plays out and you will start to believe that you deserve the better things in life and that you will obtain the things you want.

All the effort in the world will not get you what you want unless you really believe you deserve it.

Wherever you are in life and whatever you are doing remember this, you deserve to be happy and you deserve to have what you want in life. Everyone deserves happiness and joy in life, and by changing your outlook, you will change your outcome.

Start living the life you want to live, and not the life you're expected to live.

How do Millionaires Set and Achieve their Goals

"All successful achievements are the result of a predetermined goal. The goal acts as your guide – the compass that directs your course of actions to your desired result."

The Piano Principle by Brad Yates

Imagine walking into someone's home and finding the living room dominated by a beautiful grand piano. You ask your hosts for a recital, to which they reply that they don't play. As you run your hand over the sleek exterior of this magnificent instrument, you think to yourself, 'What a shame...'

I think human beings are like grand pianos - incredible creations capable of producing wonderful music. But too often that potential goes untapped. We think that greatness is meant for someone else, that we don't have the talent (the looks, the money, the time, the breaks...) And so we live lives 'of quiet desperation,' occasionally entertaining thoughts of 'What if...?'

What if Mozart had hidden his talent? (Or Bowie, or, moving from music, Edison or Gandhi, or anyone else who has made a positive difference.) I'm not saying that everyone should feel compelled to live that big, but if one has that inkling... It seems a shame that, as Oliver Wendell Holmes said, 'The average person goes to their grave with their music still in them.'

Imagine a world where people felt free to share their grandest music and make a huge positive difference. Or, at the least, were free from the negativity that causes them to hurt themselves and others. Consider what would be possible.

So, thank you for looking for ways to enhance your music-making capabilities. I encourage you to continue to make powerful choices as you reach ever-greater levels of success. I believe the purpose of life is to enjoy life, and I hope you enjoy it magnificently!

Conclusion ...

Let's hope that your path to Success and self-fulfilment is truly mind-blowing, and that the process, as well as the achievements, is positive, and energising.

Remember ...

We are programmed to survive, but really to want to do our best, and to achieve our best means some self-examination, some effort and some dedication.

Don't be fooled into thinking there are quick fixes to getting the most out of life, or that it is a question of this method or that method. The questions and the answers are always inside you, as are the unique abilities to discover and enjoy your potential.

Good Luck!

Paul Wakefield
Founder, The Wakefield Group
http://paul-wakefield.co.uk/

Paul Wakefield is the founder of the Wakefield Group

Paul has been at the forefront of Offline & Online Marketing for several years now. After spending three years working as a pub manager, eight years in the motor trade as a sales manager leading a team of eight staff, then having spent eight years as a recruitment consultant, Paul eventually started out in business in 2006 opening his first business as a recruitment agency working very closely as a consultant for the likes of Renault, Audi and Peugeot, Northumberland County Council, dfs, Biffa and Sita UK Ltd, to name a few.

Since 2009, thanks to webinars, seminars and workshops, Paul has worked with over 3,500 people from 7 different countries. In March 2013, Paul was listed as a Top 100 Marketer to follow on Twitter. Paul has recently been recognised as a SageUK Business Expert, and was also recently reward as the StartUp Britain Business Champion for Northumberland.

The Wakefield Group is made up of Paul's businesses,

1. PAULSsolutions – Consultancy & Coaching
2. Making U Social – Business events, training & workshops
3. Digital Youth Enterprise Ltd – Digital Media Trainers for young people

Paul is known as an expert in developing businesses for others and helping, supporting and inspiring them to set up small global business online.

"If you want to know how to get the most innovative offline and online business, marketing, sales and strategies that are proven to increase profits and change your life, you need to read this."